Caribbean Primary Mathematics

Level 1 Teacher's Guide

Contents

Introduction   3

  Using the *Caribbean Primary Mathematics* series   3

  Lesson planning   4

  Assessment   4

  Integration   5

  Technology   5

  Problem solving   6

  Realistic and practical activities   6

Teaching and learning materials   7

  The importance of teaching and learning materials   7

  Types of materials   8

  Resources in and around your classroom   9

  Building up a collection of materials   10

  Using materials in the mathematics classroom   12

  Using selected materials   14

  Photocopiable materials   17

  References and further reading   25

Unit-by-unit support for Pupil Book 1A   26

Unit-by-unit support for Pupil Book 1B   85

Glossary   125

Level 1 curriculum coverage grid   128

Introduction

Using the *Caribbean Primary Mathematics* series

The *Caribbean Primary Mathematics* series was originally developed and tested by members of the UWI School of Education and schools. This new edition has been revised by a pan-Caribbean team of educational experts, with the following features.

Meeting the latest curriculum objectives

We have updated the tried and tested course to meet the requirements of the latest curriculum documents from Caribbean territories. In each Teacher's Guide, you will find a grid that outlines how the curriculum objectives are covered in the course for that level. In some cases, a concept may not be required by the curricula of all the territories. You will find notes in the suggested approach for each unit pointing out which activities to leave out if they are not relevant to your students.

Up-to-date curriculum objectives

In Levels 1, 2 and 3, the series follows a spiral approach to learning. Spiralling means that every new concept is reinforced at calculated levels and extended as time goes on. Materials are organised into discrete, manageable units linked to curriculum topics.

Relevant contexts for learning

Throughout each level, you will find 'Talk about' boxes, illustrated with the CPM parrot, which provide topics for classroom discussions around topical issues relevant to the material covered on that page.

Interactive CD-Rom activities

In this new edition of *Caribbean Primary Mathematics*, each level comes with a CD-Rom packed with interactive activities for children to consolidate their learning of the key topics. There are references throughout the Teacher's Guide indicating when these activities are to be played. These are marked with the symbol .

Practical activities

Wherever you see in the Pupil Book, students have an opportunity to explore or investigate a mathematical concept through a practical, hands-on activity. If you need any resources for these activities, they will be listed under materials at the beginning of the suggested approach for that chapter.

Classroom testing and additional activities

In the Pupil's Books for this course, assessment material is provided at regular intervals giving you the opportunity to assess your students' progress and identify areas that require more practice. Additional suggestions for assessing learning are given in the unit-by-unit support.

Glossary

On pages 125–127 of this Teacher's Guide, you will find a glossary of mathematical concepts and words used in this course.

Lesson planning

It is important for you to plan your lessons before entering the classroom. Whether the plan is very detailed or only a brief outline of the activities to be carried out, it helps you to keep a record of what is to be taught. A lesson plan describes what is to be done, when it is to be done, how long it should take and what resources are needed.

One form of the lesson plan that is used widely in mathematics is known as the *Hunter Lesson Cycle*, so named because of the way the sequence of events may be repeated. The components of the *Hunter Lesson Cycle* are:

1 Set the stage.
2 State the objective.
3 Provide instructional input.
4 Model operations.
5 Check for understanding.
6 Give guided practice.
7 Give independent practice.

You may want to follow the *Hunter Lesson Cycle*, or you could use a more informal plan. Any lesson plan has three main components: the beginning, the middle and the end.

Assess readiness

Set the stage
■ Motivate

State the objective
■ Relate to prior knowledge

Provide instructional input
■ Label concepts
■ Define terms and symbols

Check for understanding
■ Ask questions
■ Observe operations
■ Reteach, if necessary

Model operations

Give guided practice
■ Students demonstrate skills
■ Students extend concepts
■ Students work examples
■ Students repeat operations

Give independent practice
■ Students practise skills

Assess mastery
■ Ask questions
■ Observe students
■ Give tests

Beginning
■ Set out the purpose of the lesson.
■ Make connections to previous lessons or material covered.
■ Initiate a participatory activity which stimulates the students' interest.

Middle
■ Introduce the mathematical concepts.
■ Demonstrate some examples of what the students are expected to do.
■ Give students time to complete their activities and tasks.
■ Assess and evaluate the students' work.

End
■ Summarise the lesson and learning activities, orally or through an activity.
■ Indicate what the follow-up to the lesson will be.

Assessment

Traditionally, assessment has comprised mainly written tests. While these are important in determining the progress of students, especially when a grade or mark is required, there are other forms of assessment that should be included in the mathematics classroom:

- questions and tasks
- practical investigations and activities
- homework
- group work
- self assessment.

In these Pupil Books, revision and assessment pages have been provided at regular intervals. These pages allow you and the students to assess how they are progressing, and to identify any areas that may need more practice.

Questions and tasks

Remember, you cannot assess all students at the same time. During any lesson, ask questions and set tasks that allow you to assess some of the students. Gradually, you will build up a clear idea of each student's progress. Make sure that the questions are clear, and that students know what they are expected to do.

Practical investigations and activities

Most practical activities require pair work or group work. The students will often have to share their answers with the rest of the class. This provides an opportunity for you to assess problem-solving and presentation skills.

Group work

Group work gives you an opportunity to assess each student's social and communication skills. More confident students will often dominate the group; always aim some questions at the shyer members of the group in order to assess their contributions too.

Self-assessment

In many cases, you can ask students to check each other's work or their own work. It is also important to ask students which parts of the lesson they found easiest or most difficult, as they often have a clear idea of the areas in which they want more practice.

Integration

Integration should be included in all aspects of mathematics instruction, both within mathematics and across mathematics and other subject areas. Firstly, within mathematics, a topic such as money cannot be introduced or reviewed without reference to related topics such as decimals, operations on numbers or place value. Secondly, many topics in mathematics are common to topics in other subject areas: measurement in science, shapes in art and map locations in social studies can all be reinforced in the mathematics classroom. Integration provides opportunities for the subject teachers to plan more effective lessons, in collaboration with other subject teachers. This helps the students to recognise that mathematics is not an isolated subject but a component of all other subjects.

Technology

Technology should form an integral part of all mathematics instruction for use by both the teacher and the student. Technology may include computers, overhead projectors, televisions, tape recorders and, of course, calculators. Computers provide immediate access to worldwide resources, visual stimuli and simulations of otherwise remote activities, and contact with learners in other places. In addition to these benefits, there are many other advantages to using technology in schools. Technology enhances the motivation of the learner in many ways. Students see technology as something fun and exciting. It immediately grabs their attention. Technology also enhances creativity as students have the opportunity to create their own materials. Each student can determine the pace at which to proceed, and thus gain more control over the learning that takes place. Technology helps the teacher to produce resources and assignments, to execute varied and interesting lessons and to store these materials efficiently over long periods. Technology is therefore an asset for both the teacher and the student.

Problem solving

Although problem solving is an integral part of mathematics instruction, many teachers teach problem solving as a separate concept. Instead, problem solving should be incorporated at all stages of the instructional process – when introducing a concept, throughout the instruction and as part of the assessment. Problem solving provides an opportunity for students to communicate, reason, explore and investigate in the mathematics classroom, thus encouraging better understanding.

There are four general stages involved in finding the solution to a problem. These are:
■ understand the problem
■ devise a plan
■ carry out the plan
■ check the solution.

There are many problem-solving strategies that may be used, depending on the problem to be solved. These include:
■ draw a diagram
■ guess and check/trial and error
■ solve a simpler problem
■ act out the problem
■ make a model
■ look for a pattern.

Realistic and practical activities

Mathematics must be taught in such a way that the students enjoy what they are doing and relate it to their everyday lives. Along with the activities suggested in the Caribbean Primary Mathematics series, you should include lessons that are realistic and practical. In addition, students must recognise the link between mathematics and their daily lives and experiences. We all use mathematics on a daily basis: we tell the time, we measure amounts when we serve and eat food, we estimate whether clothing will fit, we read maps ... just to name a few daily mathematical processes. Carpenters, painters, accountants and doctors are some of the people who depend on daily use of mathematics. For children, activities such as running races, skipping or playing card games all involve some mathematical understanding. These types of activities are ideal for teaching mathematics to ensure that all children, especially those who struggle with mathematics, become more confident and competent in their mathematical abilities.

Introduction

Teaching and learning materials

Learning aids enable students to develop their mathematical knowledge and competencies. Pupil Books and textbooks are examples of everyday learning aids. However, in order for students to gain real understanding of mathematics, they need to encounter a range of teaching and learning materials that give them practical experience in using mathematical concepts. This section tells you about the range of learning materials that you can use in your classroom. We offer suggestions about obtaining and using mathematics materials and provide information about:

- the importance of mathematical materials
- types of materials
- how to build up a collection of materials
- how to use different types of materials in your classroom
- activities related to specific learning materials.

At the end of this section, you will also find some photocopiable materials which you can copy for use in the classroom.

The importance of teaching and learning materials

Teaching and learning materials are important because they:

- engage the students in practical hands-on learning
- offer concrete examples and applications of mathematical concepts, skills and procedures
- stimulate interest, perseverance and problem-solving skills.

Each of these points is discussed in more detail below.

Combining hands-on activity with mental activity

Students learn best by doing things, by being actively engaged in the teaching/learning process. Active engagement may involve physical activity, but it should always require some form of mental activity (Anthony, 1996). For example, students may examine or use selected objects. While doing this, the students should also be required to engage in mental activities such as justifying, discussing, comparing and contrasting mathematical ideas. Learning materials facilitate practical activities which also engage students mentally.

Progressing from the concrete to the abstract

Students at the primary level are seldom able to do mathematics only at the symbolic or abstract level. Teaching and learning materials enable students to examine concepts, skills and procedures and to generalise from these examples. The materials also allow students to link the mathematical concepts to their experiences and to previous learning. Thus, teaching and learning materials can help students to learn mathematics meaningfully.

Stimulating students' interest and perseverance

Well-prepared, appropriate materials capture the students' attention, motivating them to engage with the mathematical learning process and stimulating their interest in mathematical tasks. In this way, teaching and learning materials develop students' problem-solving skills. Personal qualities – such as perseverance and willingness to engage in tasks – facilitate mathematical learning, but these qualities are also improved through the use of mathematical teaching and learning materials.

Types of materials

You can use a wide range of materials in your classroom, including found objects and materials, bought materials, second-hand items and bought products. In this section we categorise materials in two different ways:

- according to the stages of mathematical development supported by each material
- according to the form of the material.

There are many other ways of categorising materials, but this section aims to give you a broad idea of the variety of materials available.

Supporting mathematical development through materials

In this course, we recommend that students begin with concrete examples, and gradually move towards working with abstract concepts. Grossnickle, Reckzeh, Perry and Ganoe (1983) divide materials into three groups which are linked with this progression from concrete to abstract.

- Manipulatives are objects that the students can feel, touch, handle and move. Examples include dice, cards, paper, clay, string, and so on. These are linked to the concrete stage of mathematical development.
- Visual, audio and audio-visual materials require students to use their senses of sight and hearing. Visual materials involve looking or watching. Examples include pictures, diagrams and photographs. Audio materials involve hearing or listening. Examples include CDs, cassette tapes, rhymes and songs. Audio-visual materials involve a combination of watching and listening. Examples include films, videos and some computer software. These materials are linked to a semi-concrete stage of mathematical development.
- Symbolic materials represent mathematics through words, numbers and symbols. Examples include textbooks, Pupil Books, worksheets and other texts. Symbolic materials are linked to the abstract stage of mathematical development.

In order to progress from the concrete to the abstract when teaching each mathematical skill or concept, you would usually introduce the work using manipulatives. You could then gradually move towards the semi-concrete stage using audio-visual material, and finally progress towards the abstract stage using symbolic materials.

Different forms of materials

We can also categorise materials according to form. Materials take four different forms: manipulatives, print materials, games and puzzles, and technological devices. The table below outlines these forms and gives some examples of each. Remember, these categories are not mutually exclusive. For example, software packages could include games and puzzles as well as print media. However, this table is intended to give you an idea of the sheer range of materials available.

Type of material	Description	Examples
Manipulatives	Materials that students can handle, feel, touch and move	■ Real-life objects such as shells, seeds, buttons, money ■ Objects specifically designed to represent mathematical ideas e.g. geo-boards, abaci, base ten blocks, geometrical shapes or models
Print materials	Materials that convey information in words, pictures or diagrams	■ Activity cards that outline tasks ■ Pupil Books and worksheets ■ Flash cards ■ Charts
Games and puzzles	Games are activities that are guided by rules; puzzles are non-routine problems	■ Commercial games, e.g. snakes and ladders, dominoes, card games ■ Teacher- or student-made puzzles and games
Technological devices	Materials that require electronic or other technology	■ Calculators, films, videos, CDs, computer software packages

Resources in and around your classroom

Immediate resources

Your classroom is an immediate source of learning materials. Many everyday objects can be used for measurement and data collection activities, and for developing number concepts and computation strategies. Examples include:

■ parts of the classroom – floor, door, windows, board, and so on
■ furniture – desks, chairs, cupboards, shelves, and so on
■ students' possessions – pencils, rulers, pens, school bags, lunch boxes, and so on.

The school compound beyond your classroom is also a rich source of materials. Students can explore mathematical concepts such as symmetry by examining the school buildings, playground, plants and trees. The activities that take place within the school compound also provide learning opportunities. For example, students could carry out investigations to determine the most popular games, sports, lunch foods, and so on. Each school compound is different, so you should explore your school compound to determine how it can be used to teach mathematics.

A classroom bulletin board

A classroom bulletin board allows you to display work and share ideas. To set up a bulletin board, you may designate an area of wall space or use a board made of soft wood such as chipboard. Work together with your students to prepare and monitor the bulletin board displays. In Levels 1 to 3, you will need to take responsibility for maintaining the display. From Level 4 upwards, the students can take on more responsibility for preparing and maintaining the display. Use the bulletin board to:

- pose problems and puzzles
- explain solutions to displayed problems and puzzles
- elicit examples of concepts
- display the results of data collection exercises
- display pictures and examples of how mathematics is used in real life (graphs, maps, and so on).

Your students may learn from the displays independently, in their own time. However, you should actively use the bulletin board by discussing the displays with the students, and using the discussions for informal assessment purposes.

Learning centres

You can also set up a learning centre in your classroom. The learning centre is an area where you store enrichment activities and materials at varying levels of difficulty. Check and comment on students' work and provide guidance for possible follow-up activities.

Building up a collection of materials

Students are most likely to use materials that are readily available in the classroom. So it is a good idea to build up a varied collection of learning materials for your classroom.

Selecting appropriate materials

When selecting materials, ask yourself the following questions:

- Are the materials directly related to the concepts or skills being developed?
- Do the materials facilitate the students' movement from one level of abstraction to another, for example, from the concrete to the abstract?
- Are the materials appropriate for the ages and developmental level of your students?
- Are the materials big/small enough for the students to use easily?
- Does the level of complexity match your students' mathematical development and needs?
- Are the materials challenging enough/easy enough?
- Will the materials stimulate the students' interest?

The following list gives you an idea of the types of materials that could be used in teaching the various content areas. Note that the list is not exhaustive, and the assignment of materials to particular content areas is not definitive. Some materials are suitable for teaching a variety of content areas or topics, as necessary and appropriate.

Types of materials

Content areas	Manipulatives	Print materials	Games and puzzles	Technological devices
Number concepts and computation	Common objects, e.g. buttons, seeds, stones, sticks; base ten blocks; place value charts or pockets; hundred charts; sorting trays; attribute blocks; sand boxes; Cuisenaire rods; abaci (counting frames); fraction sets	Numeral and base facts; flash cards; stories with a mathematical theme; number lines	Numeral jigsaw puzzles; colour-by-number puzzles; dominoes	Calculators
Measurement	Ruler; measuring tapes; clocks; watches and watch faces; measuring cylinders; cups; spoons; thermometers; balance and scales; various containers; string; trundle wheel; simple maps; calendars; squared paper			
Money	Coins; notes; play money notes	Advertisements		Calculators
Geometry	Models of 2D and 3D shapes; geo-board; tangram pieces; drinking straws; string; attribute blocks	Dot and squared paper	Battleship game	
Statistics and data handling	Building blocks; dice	Newspaper and magazine clippings of graphs; squared paper		Graphing software

Acquiring materials

The quickest way to acquire materials is to buy them. However, this can be unnecessarily expensive. There are many inexpensive, effective ways of building up a collection of learning materials. Here are some suggestions:

- collect manipulatives such as shells, seeds, stones, sticks and beads
- prepare your own fraction pieces from sheets of card or plastic
- prepare place value charts using Bristol board
- involve parents in constructing materials such as geo-boards, sets of 3D shapes, abaci, and so on
- involve students in constructing simple materials such as clock faces, tangram pieces, equivalent fraction charts, and so on.

If you decide to construct materials, first find a well-prepared commercial or local example of the material, note its mathematical properties, and ensure that these properties are features of your constructed materials. For example, when guiding your students to construct equivalent fraction charts, ensure that the fractional parts have been divided correctly.

Whether you purchase or construct your materials, ensure that they are attractive, durable and safe to use. Protect re-usable materials from damage so that they can be used repeatedly. Laminate materials such as charts and work cards, and store all materials in a cool, dry place. You can use cardboard boxes or inexpensive plastic bins as containers.

Using materials in the mathematics classroom

You can use materials in your classroom in several ways. For example, you could use materials to:

- facilitate the use of teaching methods such as guided discovery and co-operative learning groups
- provide enrichment activities
- cater for students' individual abilities and allow them to progress at different rates
- introduce new concepts
- initiate investigations
- generate discussions.

As far as possible and appropriate, the students themselves should work with the materials – either on their own or with your guidance – in order to explore mathematical ideas. When you use the materials for demonstration or instruction purposes, make sure that you select materials that are large enough for the students to see easily.

Several factors influence how effectively the teaching or learning materials enhance students' learning. Some of these factors include:

- the students' readiness for materials
- the quality of materials
- the appropriateness of the materials for developing the mathematical ideas of the lesson.

Below you will find some general and specific guidelines for using materials in your classroom.

General guidelines

- Check your supplies. Ensure that you have sufficient materials so that each student can have the quantity of materials necessary to develop the intended concept, skill or procedure.

- Plan properly. Before the lesson, select the materials you want to use, and plan how to integrate them into the lesson. Sometimes, during the lesson, you may find that students need other materials; adjust your lesson and include the use of other materials as necessary.
- Get to know the material. Acquaint yourself with the materials before introducing them to your students. If you are unfamiliar with the materials, practise using them yourself before the lesson. Preview print material, films, videos and computer software in order to identify the mathematical concepts and vocabulary that students should have acquired in order to use the materials successfully.
- Use a range of materials. There are a variety of ways to teach each mathematical concept, skill or procedure. For example, when students are learning about place value, they could use abaci, ice-cream sticks, base ten blocks, place value charts, and so on. A variety of materials appeals to students' different interests and learning styles. Also, as students identify differences and similarities in the representations, they will gradually abstract the relevant mathematical ideas.
- Make sure students understand what to do with the materials. Let the students play with new or unfamiliar materials before you use them formally in a lesson. Ask questions to find out what they learned about the materials, and use these observations as a basis for the formal use of the materials in the classroom. Ensure that the students understand the purpose for using the materials, and how to use them.
- Evaluate the use of the materials after each lesson. Ask yourself: Were the students motivated? Did they understand what to do with the materials? What difficulties, if any, arose during the lesson? Did the materials help the students to develop the intended learning outcomes?

Guidelines for using manipulatives
- Monitor your students' progress. Allow them to work with manipulatives until they are ready to move onto semi-concrete or symbolic representations. Also remember that if you let students continue working with manipulatives for too long, they may become bored and demotivated. Always monitor your students' progress to determine the most appropriate time for them to move on to other representations.
- Ask questions. Encourage students to talk about what they are doing and understanding as they use manipulatives. Their comments may be used for assessment purposes and to guide the development of your lessons.

Guidelines for using print materials
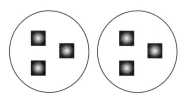
- Encourage your students to describe pictures, drawing and diagrams. They should identify components such as lines, shapes, labels, and so on. Encourage them to interpret and discuss the meanings of each component. For example, students should be able to discuss the various ways they could interpret a diagram such as the one on the left.

- Use print materials such as textbooks, Pupil Books, newspaper clippings, and so on for a variety of purposes. For example, students may use these materials as a source of information, for drills and practice exercises, or for checking generalisations they have developed.
- Use manipulatives to help students gain understanding of the mathematical ideas and vocabulary in the print material.
- Make sure that the language and instructions are clear, easy-to use and pitched at the students' level of development. The mathematical language should always be used accurately, information should be well spaced and easy-to-read, and pictures and diagrams should reinforce the ideas and make reading easier.

Guidelines for using games and puzzles
- Build up your collection of games and puzzles by encouraging students to develop their own games and puzzles. You can also develop new games by adapting rules and actions of existing games.
- Each time you play a game, make sure students understand the rules.
- Monitor your students' progress during games. Check their use of mathematical concepts or skills required by the game. Note their strengths, weaknesses and misconceptions.
- During the game or puzzle session, discuss the students' responses with them. Encourage them to explain what they learned and to identify their difficulties. Follow up with appropriate activities to help them to improve.

Guidelines for using technological devices
- Prepare your students for using technological materials. Introduce the key ideas, concepts and vocabulary they will hear, see or use.
- Use follow-up activities to review, evaluate and reinforce the mathematical ideas used in the materials.

Using selected materials

The geo-board
A geo-board is a piece of board with an array of pegs or nails securely fastened to the board. Although the sizes of geo-boards may vary, an appropriate size for students is a 20 cm × 20 cm board with five rows of five nails or pegs (for younger students) or ten rows of ten nails or pegs (for older students). They can stretch rubber bands around the nails or pegs to make different kinds of shapes.

Geo-boards may help students develop and consolidate geometrical concepts related to plane shapes, for example polygons, curves, lines and symmetry.

Activities
Ask students to make different types of shapes on their geo-boards and to describe them. For example:
- Make a four-sided figure. How many different four-sided figures can you make? Describe and name these shapes.
- Make a triangle with one right angle. Take another rubber band and make another triangle so that your first triangle changes to a rectangle. Explain what you did to make the rectangle.

- How many rectangles with an area of 24 square centimetres can you make on your geo-board? Write down the lengths of their sides.
- Make a quadrilateral whose area is the same as its perimeter. Describe your shape.

These types of activities could be followed up by activities involving drawing shapes on dotted, square, graph or plain paper.

Tangram puzzles

Tangram puzzles are made up of seven shapes cut from a square piece of paper, as shown below. Use heavy paper such as cardboard or Bristol board. If these are unavailable, use plain paper. You should provide younger students with the pieces; older students may make their own.

Instructions for making tangram pieces

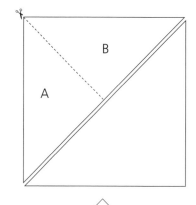

- Start with a square piece of paper.
- Fold the square in half to make two triangles. Mark the fold line with a pencil or crayon. Cut along the fold line.
- Take one of the triangles and fold it in half to make two, smaller triangles. Cut along the fold. Set aside the two triangles.

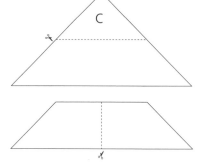

- Take the other large triangle. Place the cut edge horizontally. Take the top point and fold it down until it touches the middle of the long cut edge. Open it again. The fold should make a small triangle at the top of the paper. Cut along the fold as shown in the picture. Then place this small triangle with your other two completed pieces.
- Place the remaining piece horizontally on your desk. Fold it in half and cut along the fold line as shown.

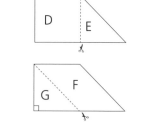

- Take one of the halves. Turn your paper so that the longest side is on the bottom. Place this side horizontally on your desk. Fold the longest side so that you get a square and a triangle. Cut along the fold line. Set aside these pieces with your other completed pieces.
- Take the remaining piece and fold it so that the 90 degree angle touches the angle opposite it. Cut along the fold line.

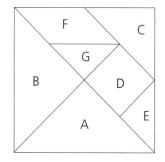

- You should now have the seven pieces of the tangram puzzle.

Activities

- Put the pieces back to form the original square.
- Name the shapes of the seven pieces.
- Make other geometrical shapes using a combination of the pieces. For example: make a triangle using two triangular pieces – E and G; make a square using three of the pieces – C, G and E; make a rectangle using four triangles and one quadrilateral – A, B, F, E and G.
- Make everyday shapes such as a boat, or a bird, using all or some of the pieces.

Worksheets

You may design worksheets in such a way that they are self-correcting. For example, you could use a puzzle in a worksheet. As the students attempt to solve the puzzle, they would get an indication as to whether their responses to the tasks are correct. If they solve the puzzle, their responses are most likely correct. The puzzle may take the form of words or phrases that the students have to complete. An example is given on the next page.

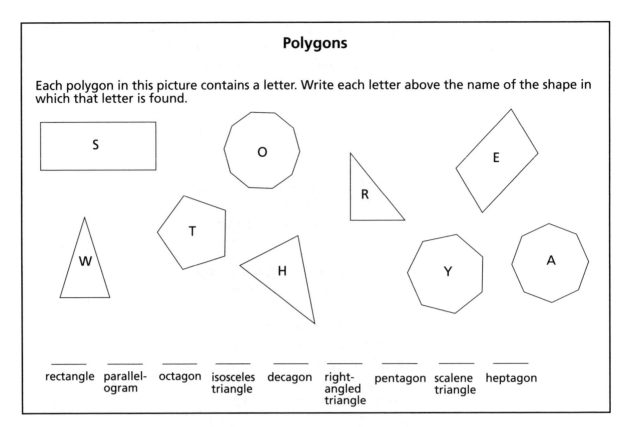

Polygons

Each polygon in this picture contains a letter. Write each letter above the name of the shape in which that letter is found.

```
____      ____       ____      ____        ____     ____        ____       ____      ____
rectangle parallel-  octagon   isosceles   decagon  right-      pentagon   scalene   heptagon
          ogram                triangle              angled                triangle
                                                     triangle
```

Calculators

Use calculators for the following purpose:

■ to investigate concepts and problems requiring computation strategies beyond the students' level

■ to build up strategies for recalling basic facts

■ to study real-life situations.

To help your students learn to use calculators sensibly, you should model the appropriate use of calculators in a variety of situations. You should also make them aware that some situations may require the use of calculators, while others may require a combination of mental or pencil-and-paper working; they should use the most appropriate strategy in a given situation.

Activities

Help your students to understand the functions of the calculator keys. For example, you could ask the students to press a key or a series of keys and note what happens on the display.

Use calculator games to help develop students' reasoning skills. Two examples are outlined below.

■ Students can work in pairs. Each student keys in a number, such as 25, into his or her calculator. Each student them uses any combination of the four operations (−, +, ×, ÷) to get an answer of 0. Multiplication by 0 and division by 0 are not allowed. The student who gets to 0 using the fewest operations is the winner.

■ Students work in pairs using one calculator per pair. They key in a number such as 100. The first player subtracts any number from 1 to 9 (including 1 and 9). The second player does the same, this time subtracting from the difference that is on the display. The players alternate turns. If a player subtracts a number to get 0, that player loses the game.

Photocopiable materials

The following are some materials that you can copy for use in your class.

Decimal paper

Decimal squares

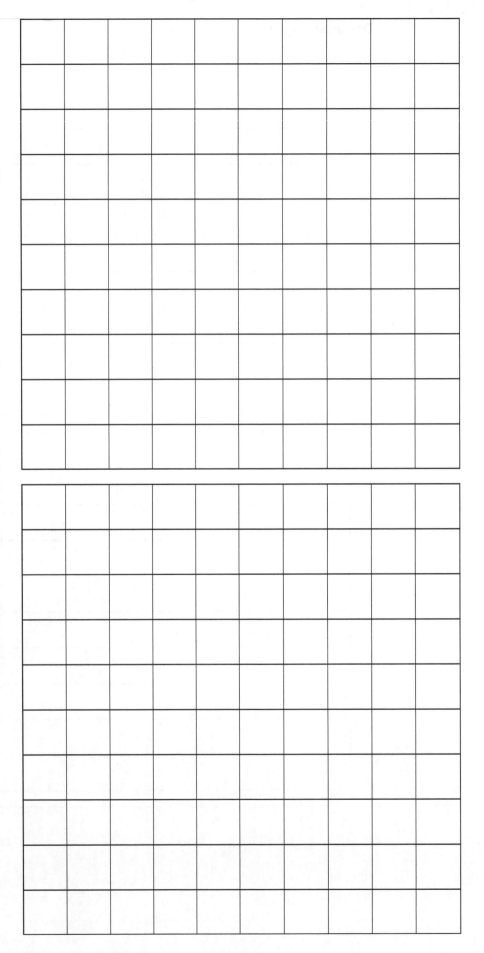

Teaching and learning materials

Clock face and hands

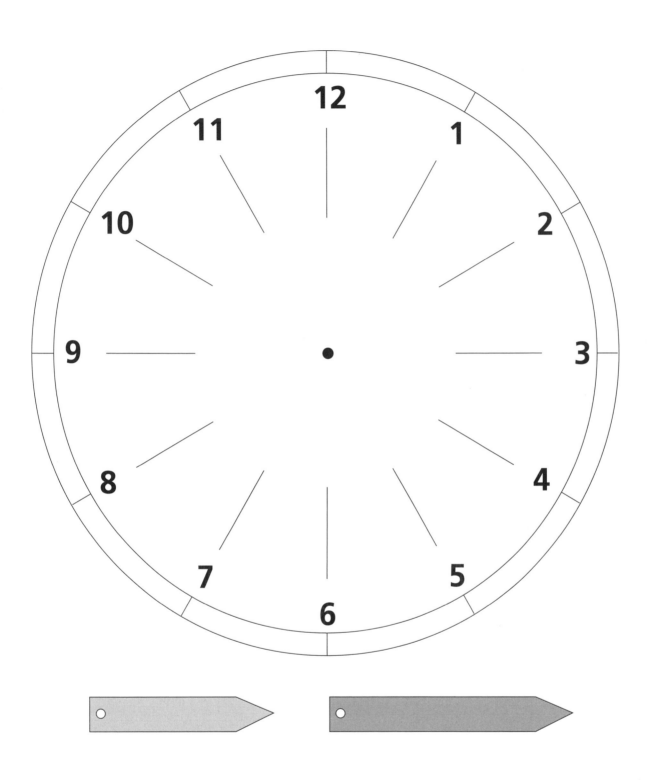

Geometric shapes

Teaching and learning materials

Centimetre squared paper

Blank number lines

Teaching and learning materials

Net for a cub die

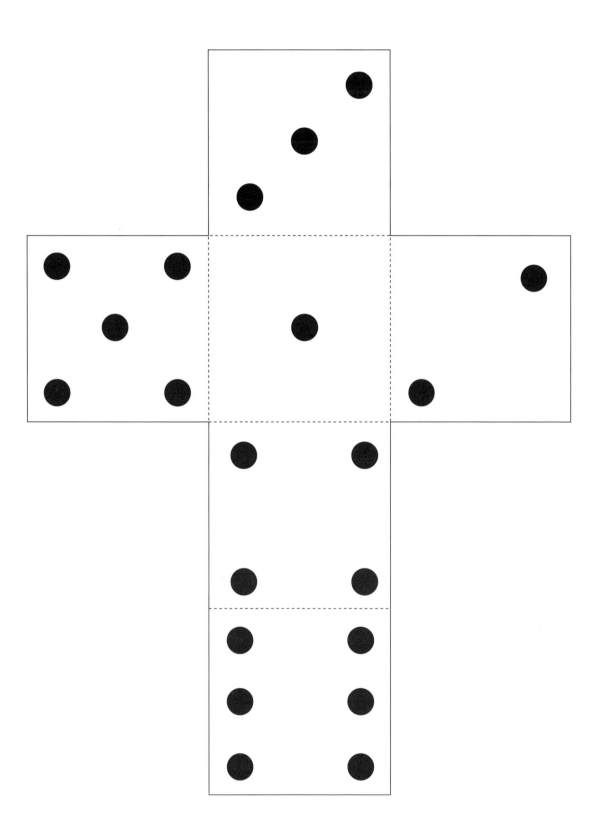

January	February	March
April	May	June
July	August	September
October	November	December

Fraction strips

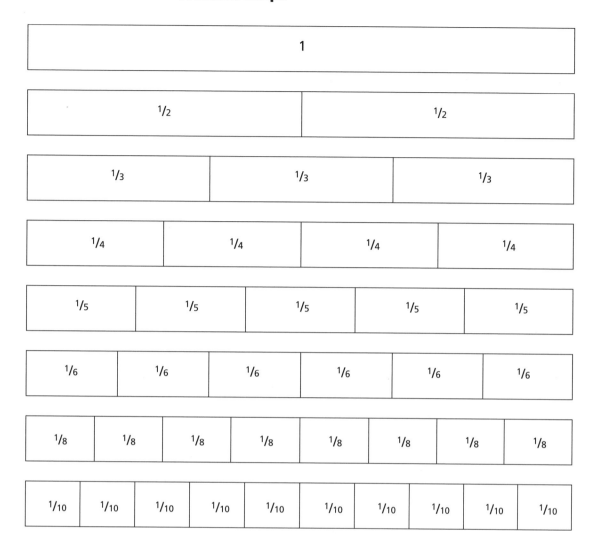

References and further reading

Anthony, G. (1996). 'Active learning in a constructivist framework', *Educational Studies in Mathematics*, 41 (3), 3–11.

Grossnickle, F.E., Reckzeh, J., Perry, L.M. & Ganoe, N.S. (1983). *Discovering meanings in elementary school mathematics* (7th ed.), New York: Holt, Rinehart & Winston.

Lemlech, J.K. (1998). *Curriculum and instructional methods for the elementary and middle school* (4th ed.), Upper Saddle River, NJ: Merrill.

Sheffield, L. & Cruikshank, D.E. (2000). *Teaching and learning elementary and middle school mathematics* (4th ed.), New York: John Wiley.

Unit-by-unit support for Pupil Book 1A

Refer to the grid on pages 128 to 132 to see how the curriculum objectives for different territories are covered in this book.

Readiness activities

Before you start working through the units, we suggest that you carry out some readiness activities with the class.

Readiness activities aim to:
- help students settle down and adjust to their new classroom environment
- enable students to practise and develop language skills, particularly in communicating mathematical ideas
- provide opportunities for students to develop early mathematical skills such as sorting, creating patterns and counting
- ensure that students realise that mathematics is an integral part of daily life
- encourage the use of mathematics in situations involving the natural integration of other subject areas
- allow you to assess students' preparedness for Level 1 mathematics.

The readiness activities suggested below are practical and fun – they aim to encourage and motivate students to produce their best.

Activity 1   Handling objects

Materials
- Small objects such as shells, pebbles, bottle-caps or seeds

Objectives
Students should be able to:
 handle manipulatives in order to make patterns and sets.

Suggested approach

Give each student a unique set of objects; vary the objects and the amount given. Allow them to play with the objects and to tell each other how they would arrange their objects in sets.

Ask the students to stand and then teach them the action rhyme *Two Little Blackbirds*:
Two little blackbirds sitting on a wall,
one named Peter, one named Paul.
Fly away Peter, fly away Paul.
Come back Peter, come back Paul.

For the actions, have the students hold up two index fingers – one represents Peter; the other represents Paul. The students make Peter and Paul appear and disappear by bending their fingers at the appropriate times in the rhyme.

Repeat the rhyme regularly over the next few lessons.

Activity 2   Patterns and numbers

Materials

- elbow macaroni or drinking straws cut into 2 cm lengths and coloured using food colouring, paint or markers
- a piece of string long enough to make a necklace, one piece per student

Objectives

Students should be able to:

 manipulate sets of small objects to form patterns

 say the number words and count to three.

Suggested approach

Give each student a piece of string and a handful of coloured objects. Show them how to thread the objects onto the string and tell them to use their own patterns to make a necklace. Do not worry that students do not count at this stage; the action of threading the beads one by one helps to develop basic ideas about number.

Play a game to help the students learn the number names. Ask them to stand with the necklaces round their necks. Then ask them to mark time to the rhythmical beat of:
"Left, right, left, right, left, right, left, right ..."

Continue to say rhythmically with them:
"See us marching with our necklaces: one, two; one, two; ..."

Change the rhyme so that the children then clap on three. Once you have finished, collect the necklaces, making a classroom display.

Activity 3   Making sets

Materials

- number or shape tray for each child (use egg trays)
- small objects (several kinds and colours for each child)

Objectives

Students should be able to:

 sort objects and put sorted objects into a specified place

 count to four.

Suggested approach

Give each student a sorting tray and some small objects. Ask questions to lead them to suggest how they could sort objects using the tray. Give them some time to sort objects using the tray. Let them tell each other what characteristics they used for sorting. At the first signs of boredom, move on.

Ask the students to stand and then ask one boy or girl to come to the front as a leader. Teach the class the following jingle and let the leader do the actions indicated by the number.
The little girl claps her hands, one;
The little girl claps her hands, one, two;
The little girl claps her hands, one, two, three;
The little girl claps her hands, one, two, three, four …

Repeat the jingle several times alternating boys and girls as the leader. Repeat with the whole class singing "We all clap our hands, one …", and so on.

Activity 4 Making sets

Materials
- number trays (one for teacher and one per student)
- small objects (several kinds and colours per student)

Objectives

Students should be able to:

 put together sets of objects with and without instruction

 practise counting to five.

Suggested approach

Give each student a number tray and a set of objects. Let them play with the number trays and objects. Observe the students as they work to see what they do.

Direct the students to put objects into the various boxes. Your directions should be very clear and they will depend on what objects you use. For example:
- Put all the black seeds in this box.
- Put all the white pebbles in this box.
- Put all the little brown shells in this box.

Play the number games from the previous lesson again but extend the numbers to five.

Activity 5 Sorting and distinguishing shapes

Materials
- shape trays (one for teacher and one per student)
- small objects from activity 4

Objectives
Students should be able to:
-  sort sets of objects
- work cooperatively
- count to six
- distinguish some simple shapes.

Suggested approach

Give each student a shape tray and a handful of objects. Show the class the three shapes on your shape tray. Say the name of each shape (circle, square, triangle) as you run your finger around the sides of each shape. Encourage the students to do the same.

Encourage the students to find examples of the shapes you have mentioned around them.

Tell the students to put a set of different objects in each shape. They will make up their sets using the objects they have ñ any grouping should be encouraged.

Repeat the number games from previous lessons extending the number range to six.

Activity 6 Many and few, counting to eight

Materials
- number trays
- an assortment of small objects
- flash cards with 'many', 'few', 'less than', 'more than', on them
- picture showing many objects
- picture showing few objects

Objectives
Students should be able to:
- make sets containing many or few objects
- say which set contains more than or less than another
- count to eight.

Suggested approach

Allow the students to play with their number trays and groups of objects to sort them as before. Ask questions to see what criteria they are using. Help any hesitant children.

Work with the whole class. Call up three children and give them a large group of objects. As you hand them out, say "I give Jane many seeds." Call up three more children and ask them to take many of an object. Display the picture showing many things and ask the students to tell you what they can see to reinforce the word "many". Repeat this whole process for "few" objects.

Ask students to work in pairs. Give one in each pair a few objects and the other many objects. Use these groups to teach more than and less than. Give each pair a chance to say "I have more than John. John has less than me."

Round off the lesson by getting the students to say and act out the rhyme:
One, two, buckle my shoe;
Three, four, knock at the door;
Five, six, pick up sticks;
Seven, eight, lay them straight;
One, two, three, four, five, six, seven, eight.

Activity 7 Making sets of many and few objects

Materials
- pictures from the previous activity
- number trays and small objects

Objectives
Students should be able to:

- make sets containing many and few objects
- say which set contains more or less than another.

Suggested approach

Direct the students to make two sets – one containing many objects, the other containing few. Check to see that they can do this.

Make a set of a few objects. Say something like: "I have three objects in my set. Is this more than or less than you have?" Repeat this using many objects.

Refer to the pictures on display. Encourage the students to tell you about the pictures using full sentences. For example: There are many cars. There are few trees.

Teach the class the following rhyme:
One, two three; One, two three;
Lift up your head, look at the tree.
What do you see? What do you see?
Leaves so many, fruits so few.

Activity 8 Matching objects

Materials
- pebbles

Objectives
Students should be able to:

- match objects
- use the phrase 'as many as'.

Suggested approach

Play a game of musical chairs with the class to reinforce the idea of one-to-one matching. Start with a chair for each child. Lead the class to the idea that they can work out that there are 'as many' chairs as children because each child has a chair. Continue to play with one less chair. The students should work out that there is not the same number of chairs as children because one child is left standing.

You can use a counting game to demonstrate one-to-one matching.

Form a group of students. Do not count them or say how many there are. Ask them to walk past you out of the room. As each one walks past, place a pebble in a jar to represent him or her.

Have the students come back into the room. As they walk past you, remove a pebble to represent each child. Ask the class how they know the same number of students returned as went out. (All the pebbles have been removed.) Repeat this but allow one or two students to stay outside. Repeat the procedure but ask the class 'How many students are missing?' They can work this out by looking at the pebbles.

Unit 1   Numbers to 5

Pupil Book page 5

Materials
- large picture number cards for teaching
- five objects per student

Objectives

Students should be able to:

 recognise the numerals from 1 to 5

 make sets representing the numerals 1 to 5.

Suggested approach

Give each student five small objects. Hold up a picture number card (from one to five) and ask them to use their objects to make a matching set. Have them say the number of objects in the set they have made.

Note that at this stage you are showing the students that each number has its own symbol. You are not yet teaching them to read the symbol or to write it.

Have the class turn to page 5. Hold up your picture number card showing three and say: This card shows three. Take three objects. Put them on the dots in row **a** in your Pupil Book. Ask: Is there one object for each dot? (Yes.) How many objects have you used? (Three.) How many dots are there? (Three.)

Repeat this using the other numbers in rows **b** to **e**. Then go back to row **a**. Ask the students to say which set of bugs has three in it. Let them circle the correct set. Encourage them to use their objects to match one-to-one if they need to. Let them complete the page. Walk around to see which students resort to concrete matching and which can match visually.

CD-Rom activity
- Counting

Unit 2 Numbers to 6

Pupil Book page 6

Materials
- large number symbol cards
- crayons

Objectives
Students should be able to:

 count in sequence up to six.

Suggested approach

Ask six students to come to the front of the class and stand facing the board. Give each student a large number symbol card from one to six chosen at random. Let the students look at the numerals given to them and then hold the cards in front of their chests. As you call each number from one to six, the student with that numeral should turn around and face the class. Ask another student to come and arrange the numerals in order from 1 to 6, from left to right.

Collect the cards from the students and repeat the activity more than once using a different set of students each time. Then collect the cards from them and put them in a random pile on your desk. Call one student to look through the pile and find the number card that says one. Let him stand facing the class with the card on his chest as before. Call on other students in succession to choose the cards that have two, three, four, five and six.

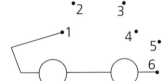

Draw a diagram like the one on the left on the board.

Ask a student to come to the board and to draw straight lines to join numerals in the correct order.

Turn to page 6. Let the students join the dots to complete the pictures. Give them some time to colour in the pictures.

In section 2, explain that the students should either write a numeral or draw objects to match the given numeral. In section 3, they should colour the correct number of objects. Check to see that they can do this before moving on.

Units 3 to 4 Seven

Pupil Book pages 7 and 8

Objectives
Students should be able to:

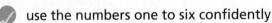 use the numbers one to six confidently

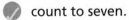 count to seven.

Draw the following on the board:

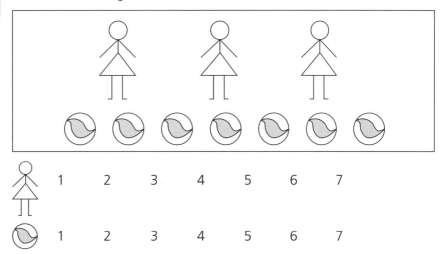

Ask a student to say how many girls you have drawn in your picture. (Three.) Point out the numerals written beside the girl below the picture. Put a circle around a numeral that shows how many girls are in the picture. (3.) Repeat this using marbles. Try to give each student many opportunities to count.

Turn to page 7. Ask: What do you see in the picture? (Cars, boys, girls, houses, and so on.) How many girls do you see? (Three.) How many boys? (Two.) How many cars? (Three.) Point out the picture of the car in row **a**. Ask again: How many cars are there in the picture? (Three.) Get everyone to circle the numeral 3. Complete the page as the class activity, getting the students to circle the numerals that show the number of girls, boys, houses, birds, trees and dogs.

Turn to page 8. Explain to the class that they are to draw lines around the objects to make sets of seven objects. It does not matter whether the objects are the same or not. What matters is that each set contains seven objects. Walk around and check that each student can do this.

Unit 5 More numbers

Pupil Book page 9

> ### Objectives
> Students should be able to:
> - use the numerals from 0 to 7 confidently
> - count sets of objects up to seven.

Suggested approach

Use this page as a continuous assessment activity to see whether the students can meet the objectives stated above. Before the students complete section 3, ask them to name the vegetables shown in the photographs.

Pupil Book page 10

> ## Objectives
>
> Students should be able to:
>
> extend their knowledge of numerals and counting in sequence up to nine.

Suggested approach

Teach the class the new numerals 6, 7, 8, and 9 in the same way as before. Pay particular attention to the correct way of forming these new numerals.

Draw a set of five circles on the board in the pattern shown below. Write the numerals 2, 3, 4, 5, 6, 7, and 8 beside the circles.

Point to the first two circles and ask a child: How many circles are there? (2.) Say: Count them all, then tell me how many there are altogether. (Five.) Encourage the students to begin counting at two, saying: Two, three, four, five. Then ask them to put a circle around the correct numeral.

Repeat with other examples and other students, always breaking the pattern of objects so that students can learn to start counting at numbers higher than one. Repeat this procedure frequently in future lessons.

Turn to page 10. Let the students trace the dot-to-dot picture with their fingers before they do it in pencil. Give them some time to colour the picture in.

Use section 3 to give practice in writing the numerals. Check to see that the students can manage. If necessary, allow them to practise further by writing pages of numerals in the exercise books.

Unit 7 Matching

Pupil Book page 11

Objectives

Students should be able to:

- extend their knowledge of numerals
- counting in sequence up to ten
- recognise the numeral for a given set.

Suggested approach

Let students say the sequences of numerals, for example 4, 5, 6, 7. This reinforces number order. If necessary, model each set using small objects in a one-to-one correspondence and have students count them.

Teach the class to write 10 in the same way as you did before. Pay particular attention to the correct way of forming the new numerals. Turn to page 11. Explain that each set on the left matches a numeral in the column on the right. Instruct students to count the objects in each set, find a matching numeral, and draw a line to join the set to the numeral. Check the completed work to see that they are able to match numerals with sets of up to ten objects.

Units 8 and 9 Adding

Pupil Book pages 12 and 13

Materials
- small objects to use as counters

Objectives

Students should be able to:

- combine sets to make amounts to ten
- write number sentences to represent addition sums.

Suggested approach

Draw a diagram like the one below.

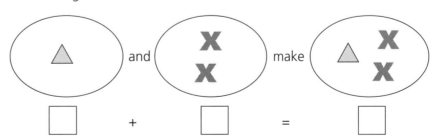

Point to the set containing a triangle and ask a student: How many in this set? (One.) Point to the two crosses and say: And how many in this set? (Two.) Ask the student to put the sets together and draw them. Let the student draw a triangle and two crosses in the empty set. Point again to the sets and say: One and two make three. Let the students write numerals in the boxes to complete the number sentence. They should read the sentence aloud.

Proceed in the same way with several more examples, in each case helping the students to:
- complete the picture sentence correctly
- read the picture sentence
- write the number sentence
- read the number sentence.

By following this pattern, you enable the students to work from specific examples towards a general understanding of number combinations. Tell the students to turn to page 12 and to complete the examples. Allow students to model the sets with counters.

CD-Rom activity
- Addition to 10

Turn to page 13. If necessary, model some more examples like those above on the board. In this activity the words 'and' and 'make' have been replaced with the symbols + and =. This forms the basis for writing proper number sentences in acceptable algorithms.

Units 10 and 11   Addition

Pupil Book pages 14 and 15

Objectives
Students should be able to:
- apply their knowledge of combining sets to make ten or less
- review basic addition facts
- understand the commutative property of addition.

Suggested approach

Talk about the picture on Pupil Book page 14. Discuss how many objects are in each set. Have the students colour the objects in each set. Let the students write how many are in each set. Once the students have completed the work, check the answers with them and discuss their answers.

Draw this on the board:

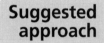

$$3 + \boxed{} = 7$$
$$4 + \boxed{} = 7$$

Point to the black squares and say: How many squares can you see? (Seven.) Count them. Then point to the first number sentence and ask: What does this say? (It says three and another number make seven.) How can we find the other number? Let a student come to the board and show how the other number can be found. The drawing on the board should look like one of those below.

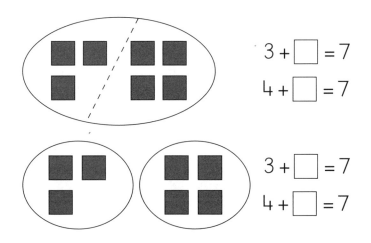

$3 + \square = 7$

$4 + \square = 7$

$3 + \square = 7$

$4 + \square = 7$

Ask: How many objects are in this set? (Three.) How many are in the other set? (Four.) Allow a student to complete the number sentence and read it aloud. Repeat the procedure for the second number sentence. Draw this on the board:

$8 = 5 + \square$

$8 = 3 + \square$

Repeat the first step above. Then continue with further examples such as:

$6 = 4 + \_\_\_;$ $9 = 3 + \_\_\_$
$6 = 2 + \_\_\_;$ $9 = 6 + \_\_\_$

Turn to page 15. Allow the students to complete the activity independently. A few students may need help with the last questions. You may find it useful to form a group of the students who need help with every exercise so that you can give them specialised attention.

Units 12 and 13   Position

Pupil Book pages 16 and 17

Materials
- alphabet bricks arranged randomly in a 5 × 5 vertical block on the table
- a box, or other small container

Objectives

Students should be able to:

- identify the position of objects presented in concrete and pictorial form
- position objects according to descriptions of their relative positions.

Suggested approach

Point to the bricks and tell the students that the bricks are on the table. Pick one brick from the arrangement and place it under the table. Tell the students that the brick is *under* table.

Stand in front of the table and tell the students that you are *in front* of the table. Repeat, but this time, stand *behind* the table.

Point to the bottom row of alphabet bricks. Say the letters together as you point to each one, for example *a, x, t, v, b*. Repeat for the other rows.

Write 'above' on the board. Demonstrate one letter being positioned above another by pointing. For example *c is above p*.

Choose a letter, for example q. Ask a student to name a letter that is directly above q. Repeat, choosing a different student each time.

Repeat with the words 'next to' and 'in'. You will need to use the box or container to demonstrate 'in'.

Ask students to describe the position of a brick in relation to another brick or another object. For example: *Where is q in relation to p?* Students should then say whether q is on, under, next to, above behind, or in front of brick p.

Instruct the students to complete Pupil Book pages 16 and 17.

Unit 14   Days of the week

Pupil Book page 18

Materials
- day cards (Monday to Sunday), one for each child
- line and pegs

Objectives
Students should be able to:
 name the days of the week
 state the number of days in a week.

Suggested approach

Give one day card to each child in order. Say the day written on the card as you present it.

Ask the students to sort themselves into groups with the same day.

Chant the days of the week, starting at Monday. As you say each day, ask all the students in that group to stand up. Continue in order through to Sunday, until all the students are standing up.

Repeat the chant, but this time the groups of students sit down.

Choose a student holding 'Monday' to peg it on the line, to the left. Ask the class what day comes after Monday. (Tuesday.) Choose a student holding a Tuesday card to peg it to the right of Monday. Continue like this until the seven days are arranged on the line.

Chant the days in order with the students as you point to each card.

Ask the students what day it is today (for example Tuesday). Point to Tuesday on the line. *The say before today was Monday. The day after today is Wednesday. Wednesday is tomorrow.*

Instruct the students to complete Pupil Book page 18.

Unit 15 Months of the year

Pupil Book page 19

Objectives

Students should be able to:

 name the months of the year

 state and write the current date of the current day.

Suggested approach

Point to each month card pegged on the line in order, saying them aloud. Repeat with the students joining in.

Choose a student to point to any month on the line. Ask the class which month is being pointed to (for example April). Ask the students which month comes before it. (March.) Point to the month on the line. Ask the students which month comes after April. (May.) Point to the month on the line.

Choose another student to point to their favourite month. Ask the student why it is their favourite month (for example September). Ask the class which month comes before September and which month comes after September.

Repeat several times.

Ask the students what a calendar shows. (The calendar shows the names of the months, the days of the weeks and their dates.) Let them look at the calendar to check their answers. Display the outline of a calendar, and write the names of the days at the heads of the columns. Ask: 'Who knows what today's date is?' Let the students tell you if they can. Get a student to write the date on the board. Explain that the date tells us two things: what month it is, and how many days we have had in the month.

Ask the students to name the current month. Write it on the calendar in the space above the days of the week. Ask again what is the number of today's date, pick out that numeral from among those you have cut out for the lesson (or from the number card pack), and stick it in the correct place in the outlines. Show the students how they can see what day of the week it is by looking at the column in which you have pasted the date.

Instruct the students to complete page 19 of Pupil Book A.

Unit 16   Empty sets

Pupil Book page 20

Materials
- a large number of bottle-caps

Objectives

Students should be able to:

 understand the concept of an empty set

 recognise and write 0.

Suggested approach

Arrange the students in pairs and give six bottle-caps to each pair. Let one child in the pair distribute the bottle-caps one at a time between the pair.

When all the pairs have done this, have the students put their bottle-caps on their books. Ask them to remove one. Repeat this till they have removed all three. Ask: Are there any bottle-caps left on your book? (No.) Say: When there are no things in a set, the set is empty.

Draw a set of five objects on the board. Ask: How many objects are in the set? (Help the students to count them.) Let the class suggest what you should do to make this into an empty set. (Remove the five objects.) Erase the objects and then say: This is an empty set. There is nothing in it.

Turn to page 20. Tell the class what is happening in each picture. (All the cookies are eaten. All the birds have flown away. All the pencils have been given out.) In each case, ask: How many are left? (None.)

Tell the class that none in maths can be written as zero. Let them practise writing 0 as they did with other numerals.

Complete the writing task on page 20 after the class has had some practise writing 0.

Units 17 and 18   Ordering numbers and number lines

Pupil Book pages 21 and 22

Materials
- collection of small objects for counting
- number line tape
- clothes pegs
- number symbol cards 0 to 10

Objectives

Students should be able to:

 recognise the number sequence from zero to ten

 distinguish between odd and even numbers

 represent amounts on a number line.

Suggested approach

This is the first time that students formally come into contact with the terminology 'odd and even'. You will need to teach them what we mean when we talk about odd and even numbers. Walk around the class and give each group of students an arbitrary amount of marbles, pebbles, shells or other small objects. Instruct the groups to arrange the objects into groups of two. Some groups will have one object left over. Ask the groups who have managed to make smaller groups of two with none left over to put up their hands. Let them count the objects in twos and say how many they have. Write these numbers on the right-hand side of the board. Ask the groups that have one object left over to put up their hands and repeat this procedure. Write their numbers on the left-hand side of the board. Point out that the numbers on the right-hand side of the board are even numbers, and the numbers on the left-hand side of the board are odd numbers.

Draw small groups of shapes on the board, some with an odd amount and some with an even amount. Ask individual students to count the objects in twos and to say whether each set is odd or even.

Place the number cards on a desk. Let two students hold up the clothes line in front of the class. Invite one student to take any number card and to place it on the number line. The students then take turns to select number cards and to place them in the correct sequence on the number line. You might like to reinforce odd and even by asking them to say whether the number on the card they have chosen is an odd or even number.

Turn to page 21. The first activity requires the students to fill in the missing numbers on the number lines. The second activity requires them to draw lines to join the number symbols in the shapes to the correct points on the number line. In the last activity, students are asked to colour odd shapes blue and even shapes red and then to complete the additional task of writing the numerals in the correct sequence on the number line.

Draw a number line on the board with eleven points on it. Label them from zero to ten. Then draw six circles on the board and ask the students to count them. Ask one student to come to the board and circle the number that says how many circles there are. Repeat with four and eight circles. Now remove the numerals from the number line so that it looks like this:

Draw seven circles. Let the students count them, and ask a student to come to the board and write the numeral 7 in the correct place on the number line. Repeat with other examples.

Turn to page 22. The students should insert the numbers on the number lines, then circle the correct numeral to show how many objects there are in each set.

Unit 19 Looking back

Pupil Book page 23

Objectives

Students should be able to:

- use the symbols > and = in number sentences
- add two one-digit numbers
- position objects according to descriptions of their relative positions
- name the days of the week
- name the months of the year
- state and write the date of the current day.

Suggested approach

This is a review lesson, which covers the skills and knowledge taught in the preceding units.

Read the instructions to the class. Let the students attempt the questions. Give guidance only as necessary. When the students have completed the Pupil Book page, discuss each of the questions and answers with them.

Note which students have difficulty and reinforce or reteach concepts as necessary.

Unit 20 How much have you learned?

Pupil Book page 24

Objectives

Students should be able to:

- identify the number of objects
- add two one-digit numbers
- identify the relative position of objects presented in pictorial form
- name the months of the year.

Suggested approach

This is an assessment lesson in which the students are tested on the concepts taught in the previous units.

Read the instructions to the class, so they all know what they have to do. When the students have completed the Pupil Book page, discuss each of the questions and answers with them.

Note which students have difficulty. You may want to give these students extra practice with these concepts.

Unit 21 Make equal sets

Pupil Book page 25

Materials

- a collection of about 20 of the same objects for teaching
- about ten small objects per student
- a large chart similar to page 9

Objectives

Students should be able to:

- make and match equal sets of objects
- use the word 'set' when referring to a group of objects
- use the = sign correctly and understand its meaning.

Suggested approach

Draw a set of four shapes on the board. Ask the students to use their own objects to make a set that has as many objects as the one on the board.

Check to see that this has been done correctly. Repeat the procedure using different numbers of shapes and objects until you are sure that the students understand what they are doing.

Draw two sets like the ones below on the board:

Draw sets A and B on the board.

A.
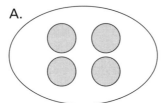

B.
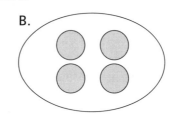

Question the students until they say that A and B have the same number of objects. Draw an equals sign (=) between the sets. Explain that we use the equals sign to show that two sets have the same number of objects.

Draw sets C and D.

C.
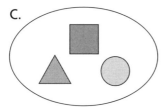

D.
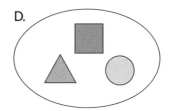

Repeat the procedure followed above but have the students match the objects to corresponding objects (triangle to triangle, and so on).

Have the students complete page 25. Point out that there is an equals sign between each pair of sets so they must draw sets that are equal in objects. It is likely they will draw the same shapes as those given, but it is not necessary for them to do this.

Check the completed Pupil Book pages to ensure that all students can make and match equal sets. Make a note of those who struggle and give them additional practical support when you get the chance.

Additional activities

For additional practice in matching sets, you can make up similar activities to those on Pupil Book page 25, using elements such as shapes (squares, circles, triangles, rectangles), fruits (apples, bananas, pears, and so on), and different faces (smiling face, sad face, surprised face, and so on). If you wish, use cut-outs of shapes, fruits and different faces so that you can easily make up sets on a board by sticking selected elements in sets.

- Draw one set, and have the students draw one to match.
- Stick up a set, and then hold up cut-outs one by one, letting the students say whether each picture matches one in the set.
- Stick up one set of objects, and ask a student to select cut-outs and stick up a matching set. Let the other students correct the answer, if necessary.
- Have students make up their own matching sets using cut-outs or objects.

Unit 22 One more

Pupil Book page 26

Materials
- square grid (10 × 10 squares)
- 15 paper circles
- bottle-caps

Objectives

Students should be able to:

 begin to grasp the concept of 'one more than'.

Suggested approach

Place the square grid so that all the students can see it. Build up a set of steps as shown below. Ask the students to say what they notice about the 'steps' working from the top to the bottom. (Each step has one more circle that the one before it.)

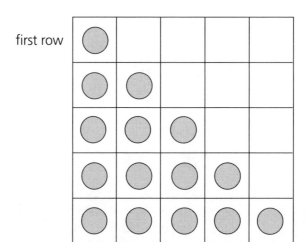

first row

Count the circles in each step. Make sure the students can see that each step is one more than the previous one by removing a circle to make the steps equal and then replacing it.

Help the class draw circles on squared paper to make their own charts if possible.

Give each student eleven bottle-caps. Draw a set of two objects on the board. Say: Use your bottle-caps to make a set with the same number of objects. When this is done, say: Make another set with one more bottle-cap in it. The students should now have two sets each – one with two objects and one with three objects. Let them tell you that the second set has three objects. Repeat this with other numbers up to five. Let them count the objects in each set.

Draw a set of two objects on the board. Say: Use your bottle-caps to make a set that has more than this set. The students should make a set of three objects. Repeat this with other numbers up to ten. Include the empty set and see if students realise that one more than zero is one. Go round the class helping those students who need assistance.

Turn to page 26. Read the instructions carefully and ensure that the students understand what to do. Once they have matched the sets by colour, have them write the number of objects in the sets on the right.

Unit 23   One less

Pupil Book page 27

Materials
- 15 food cans or other large objects
- square grid and 15 paper circles

Objectives
Students should be able to:

 review 'one more than'

 begin to grasp the concept of 'one less than'.

Suggested approach

Tell the students that you are going to collect some Pupil Books. Collect four Pupil Books. Ask the class to tell you how many books you have collected.

Now ask a student to collect some Pupil Books from other children. They must take one more than the number you took. The rest of the class must watch carefully to see that the student collects five Pupil Books. Arrange the books on a desk and match the two sets. Repeat the activity for five and six Pupil Books.

Put five cans in a row on a desk. Ask a student to make another row with one less, beside the row of five cans. Ask another student to count the cans in each of the two rows. Let the students continue making rows until the pattern looks like the one on the left. Let student count each new set as it is made.

By adding an extra can to the second row and taking it away again, show that the second row is the same as the first with one can taken away, that is, with one less. Demonstrate that the same is true for the other rows.

Put the square grid on the board. Place five circles in the first row. Ask a pupil to make a row with one less in the next row. Continue in this way until there is a row of one circle.

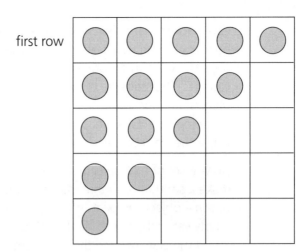

first row

Let different students count the number in each row.

Ask the students questions such as: What is one less than eight? (Seven.) Let students draw this on squared paper. Repeat a number of times, each time asking the students to subtract 1 from a number that is 10 or less.

Turn to page 27. Read the instructions with the students. Make sure they understand that they are to colour one set only. Have them complete the activity.

Unit 24   One more, one less

Pupil Book page 28

Objectives

Students should be able to:

 demonstrate their understanding of equal and unequal sets

 make sets according to given criteria.

Suggested approach

Use this page to assess whether the students understand the concept of one more and one less. Check to see that they have made the sets correctly. Assist those children who struggle with the concept.

Units 25 to 27 Using signs (>, < and =)

Pupil Book pages 29 to 31

Materials
- flash cards with signs (>, <, =)
- small objects for matching pictures

Objectives

Students should be able to:

- match objects in two sets to see which has more
- match objects in equal sets
- use the =, < and > signs correctly.

Suggested approach

Draw two sets of shapes on the board.

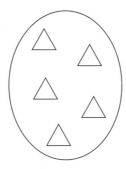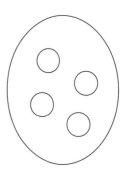

Let the students tell you ways of finding out which set has more. Remind them that one way is by drawing lines to match the shapes until no more lines can be drawn from one set. The set with the extra shapes has more. Position the flash card between the sets as shown below.

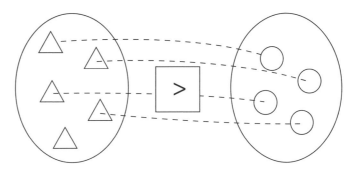

Erase the drawing and remove the flash card. Draw the sign on the board and let the students trace it in the air. Allow several students to come up and draw the sign on the board.

Repeat the exercise a few times making sure that the set with more is to the left. Let students come up and fill in the sign between the sets.

Repeat the activity above using equal sets. Remind the class that sets with the same number of objects are called 'equal sets'. Let them draw equals signs in their books and on the board.

Turn to page 29. Have the class complete the activity by filling in the signs. Encourage them to model the sets using matching objects. Complete the activities one by one, giving help to individuals who need it.

Let the students recite and act out this rhyme:
One, two, three, four, five
Once I caught a fish alive.
Six, seven, eight, nine, ten
Then I let it go again.
Why did you let it go?
Because it bit my finger so.
Which finger did it bite?
This little finger on the right.

Place the students in pairs. Give each pair several small objects in a bag. Say: I want one student in each pair to close their eyes and take out a few objects from the bag. Give the pairs a chance to talk about the objects that were removed from the bag.

Next, have the other member of the pair take objects from the bag to make a set equal to the one that his or her partner made.

Repeat this exercise once or twice.

Draw a set like the one below on the board:

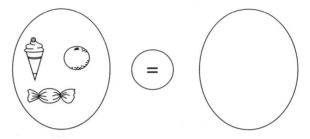

Ask the students to count the objects in the set. Let them read the sign and ask what it tells you about the second set. (It must have the same number of objects in it.) Let one student come up and draw the same number of objects.

Draw a different set on the board.

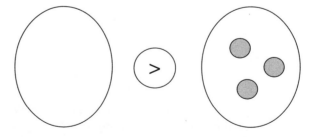

Let the students count the objects in the second circle and draw their attention to the greater than sign. Ask them what this tells us about the first set. (It must contain more objects.)

Repeat this a few more times.

Turn to page 30. Let the students talk about the sets and what the signs tell them. Let them make sets with small objects before they work in pencil. Check that they are correct and once you are sure they are able, let them draw the correct sets. Note that a variety of answers can be correct for the 'greater than' sets.

Repeat the procedure detailed above for less than signs. Remember to put the set with fewer objects on the left at this stage.

Have the students complete the activities on page 31.

Additional activities

- Give the students two numbers, such as three and seven. They must name three numbers which are bigger than three and less than seven. Repeat this activity, letting the students take turns to choose the numbers.
- Tell the students that you have a number less than twelve in your pocket. They have three chances to guess what the number is. You will only answer 'yes' or 'no'. For example, they may ask 'Is it less than ten?' and so on. When they have guessed your number, they can take turns to choose a number. You can repeat this activity at higher levels when students can ask questions such as 'Does it have two digits?', 'Is it an odd number?' and so on.

Units 28 and 29   Equal and unequal sets

Pupil Book pages 32 and 33

Materials

- assorted objects such as shells, pebbles, seeds, bottle-caps for each student
- shape tray for each student

Objectives

Students should be able to:

- develop further the concept of unequal sets
- practise making equal sets
- develop their concept of an empty set.

Suggested approach

Give each child a set of bottle-caps and a set of shells; the number of bottle-caps should be greater than the number of shells. Ask the children to put the bottle-caps in the circle of the shape tray and the shells in the square. Ask: Who can tell me something about these two sets? (There are more bottle-caps than shells.) Say: Remove all the objects and put them aside. Now take them again, one at a time, to make two equal sets on the shape tray, one set in the circle and one in the square.

Supervise this activity very closely to ensure that the two sets the children have made are equal; that is, for each object in one set there is a matching object in the other set.

Draw these two sets on the board:

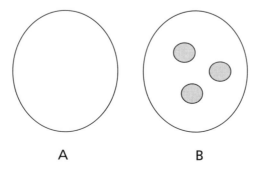

A   B

Ask: how many objects are in set A? (None.) What is the special name for a set like A? (It is an empty set.) How many objects are in set B? (Three.)

Call a student to the board and ask him or her to draw crosses to match set A to set B. Let the students talk about the equal sets.

Draw another object in set A. Ask: How many objects are now in the first set? (Four.) Are the two sets now equal? (No.) Has set A more than set B now? (Yes.) What sign should be written between the two sets? Let a student write > between the two sets. Work through another example on the board.

Turn to page 32. Tell the students that they can make crosses to represent the objects in the sets. Observe them as they work to make sure they can do it correctly.

Turn to page 33. Use this page to see whether the students can use the >, < and = signs. Observe them as they work and assist those students who need help. The 'talk about' box asks how the students can remember what < and > mean. A useful technique is to draw crocodiles with the < or > symbol forming the mouth. The mouth will always open towards the bigger 'meal' (the largest number).

Unit 30 Shapes

Pupil Book page 34

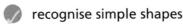

> **Objectives**
>
> Students should be able to:
> - recognise simple shapes
> - use colours to classify objects
> - recognise use of shapes in natural and human contexts.

Suggested approach

Revise the shape names with the class. Make sure they understand that the colours at the top of the page are a key for colouring the clown. You can check this by asking: What colour will we use to colour triangles? (Red.)

Let them find and colour all the triangles. Check that they have the correct colour and that they are applying their matching skills to find triangles. You could then let the students check each other's work.

Complete the rest of the colouring activity. Walk around to check that students are doing this correctly. Focus on the correct colouring of matching shapes but do not worry if the students cannot completely stay within the lines at this stage.

The 'talk about' box on page 34 encourages the students to find examples of shapes in the environment. This should provoke a great deal of classroom discussion and it offers an opportunity for you to assess verbal skills. Encourage the students to show you shapes and to say what each shape is as they find it.

Unit 31 Sorting and counting

Pupil Book page 35

Materials
- large number symbol cards showing numerals 1 to 5
- sheets of paper with one to five objects shown on them
- numeral cards from 1 to 5 for each student
- scrap paper for drawing

Objectives
Students should be able to:

 write the numerals from 1 to 5

understand the meaning of each numeral.

Suggested approach

Unit 31 can be used to review numerals from 1 to 4. The procedure is slightly different as this lesson combines previous work on making sets and counting objects with writing numerals. Have the students draw lines to make groups of shapes that are the same. Revise the shape names if you need to.

Point to the shape in 2**a**. Ask: What shape is this? (Square.) Ask the students how they know it is a square. (It has four sides that are the same length.) How many squares are there in the big picture? (Three.) Say: Write the numeral 3 below the square. Repeat this for the other shapes. Each time ask them what the characteristics of each shape are.

Have the students make their own sets of shapes and let them count each other's and write how many there are.

Unit 32 Sorting

Pupil Book page 36

Materials
- large block graph for display
- coloured squares to stick onto graph

Objectives
Students should be able to:

 classify shapes

 present information on a bar graph.

Suggested approach

Revise the names of the shapes. (Rectangle, circle, triangle, square.) Ask how many there are of each shape in turn. Let the students count and confirm each other's answers.

Move on to the large display graph. Ask the class how you could show how many of each shape there are. There are three rectangles. Place three coloured squares on the grid in the rectangles column. As you place a square of paper, say: This represents one rectangle. Repeat the procedure for the other shapes to complete the graph.

Have the students complete their own graphs on page 36.

Ask questions to make sure that they can read the graph. For example:
- How many circles are there?
- Which shape is there most of?
- How do you know?
- Which shape is there least of?
- How do you know?
- How many more circles are there than triangles?

Check the completed graphs to see that the students are able to fill them in correctly.

Unit 33 Adding 0

Pupil Book page 37

Materials
- small objects to use for demonstration

Objectives
Students should be able to:

 understand the concept of zero

 perform addition sums involving zero.

Suggested approach

Adding zero can be difficult for young children. The students need to understand that zero is the same as nothing and that adding zero, or nothing, does not change the value of the original set. The students will need lots of practice with examples where zero is involved. Demonstrate what it means to add nothing to a set showing real examples. For example, place three objects in one of your hands and none in the other. Ask the students: How many in this set? (Three.) How many in this other set? (None, or 0.) What happens if I put these two sets together? (You still have three.) Say: Yes, three plus nothing is equal to three. Repeat using different examples and amounts.

When you are satisfied that the students understand that adding nothing does not change the value of the set, show them how to represent this as number sentences. For example:
$3 + 0 = 3$ and $0 + 8 = 8$.

Turn to page 37. Discuss what is happening in the examples and read out the number sentences. Let the students complete the additions on their own. Walk around and assist any students that are struggling, praise those who are doing well.

The 'talk about' box on this page can be used to reinforce counting but also to reinforce adding 0. For example, you can say things like how many people are in this family? How many will there be if no more people join them? And so on. Let the students answer the questions.

Units 34 and 35 Subtracting

Pupil Book pages 38 and 39

Materials
- five bottles to use for demonstration
- five small objects and a shape tray per student

Objectives
Students should be able to:
- recognise subtraction as a taking away process
- use the minus or subtraction sign (–)
- perform simple subtraction with numbers less than five.

Suggested approach

Place four bottles on the desk and say: Watch closely so you can tell me what I'm doing. Slowly and deliberately take three bottles away from the four. Ask: What did I do? (You took three bottles away.) Say: Yes, that's right, I took three bottles away from the group of four. How many do I have left? (One.)

Demonstrate how to write this as a number sentence. Draw four bottles on the board. Write the numeral 4 below the bottles. Remind the class that you took three bottles away. Teach them that we use the minus sign to show take away and write the sign after the four. Cross out three of the bottles. Say: We took away three so we write the numeral 3 after the subtraction sign. Complete the number sentence. The drawing on the board should look like the one on the left.

$$4 - 3 = 1$$

Do the following examples in the same way:
$$5 - 2 = 3$$
$$3 - 1 = 2$$

Each of the pictures on Pupil Book page 38 illustrates the subtraction process. For example, ten ducks moving away leaving four behind; seven sleeping cats with two waking up and moving away. Because the students may not understand what the pictures portray, each should be discussed in detail before the students complete the activity.

Give each student five small objects and a shape tray. Say: Put three objects in the circle. Take away one and put it in the triangle. How many are left in the circle? (Two.) Let a student go to the board and write the number sentence (3 − 1 = 2). Let the class read the number sentence aloud. (Three take away one equals two.) Repeat this using the examples from the Pupil Book.

Turn to page 39. As in the previous unit, discuss the meaning of each picture before letting the students do the computation, write the number sentence and read it aloud. Go round the class asking individuals about the meaning of the pictures, helping them to write their number sentences, and listening to them as they read the number sentences aloud.

Unit 36 More number sentences

Pupil Book page 40

> ### Objectives
> Students should be able to:
> partition and combine sets of up to nine objects.

Suggested approach

On the board, draw a large picture of a shape tray (that is, a circle, a triangle, and a square). Ask a student to draw three crosses in the circle. Then let them draw one cross in the triangle, and two in the square. Ask: How many crosses are in the triangle? (One.) How many are in the square? (Two.) How many does that make in all? (Three.) Is that the same number as they are in the circle? (Yes.) Say: Yes, three equals one plus two. Write this as a number sentence below the diagram.

Ask the student to read the number sentence you have just written. Then repeat the procedure with other students, using number combinations for numbers up to nine, ensuring each time that the number sentence is read aloud correctly. Encourage the students to use the empty set sometimes, for example, 9 = 9 + 0.

Do not discuss the Pupil Book page immediately with the class. Rather let them work in groups with similar exercises and worksheets before letting them complete page 40. When they do complete the page, walk around to check that they are able to partition and combine sets correctly. You could use this as a continuous assessment activity.

Unit 37 Making number sentences

Pupil Book page 41

> ### Objectives
> Students should be able to:
> - recognise shapes
> - write simple number sentences.

Suggested approach

Turn to Pupil Book page 41. Let the students colour in the shapes. Check the colouring with them. Then, let them work in pairs to count the shapes and write how many there are. Check these answers before moving on to the number sentences.

Unit 38 Operations on number lines

Pupil Book page 42

Materials
- six large objects for counting

> ### Objectives
> Students should be able to:
> - recognise the number sequence from zero to ten
> - represent amounts on a number line
> - use a number line to add and subtract.

Suggested approach

Draw a number line on the board and number it from zero to ten. Above it draw two circles and three squares. Say: Count the circles. (One, two.) As the students count, match the first circle with the numeral 1 on the line and the second circle with the numeral 2. Then say: Count the squares. (One, two, three.) Match these with the next three numerals on the number line. Then say: How many circles? (Two.) How many squares? (Three.) How many objects altogether? (Five.)

Point out that the last of the squares is matched to the numeral 5 on the number line. Let one of the students write the corresponding number sentence (2 + 3 = 5) on the board and read it aloud.

Repeat with similar examples. End with a drawing showing four circles and four crosses. This time, when the students count the circles, draw a curved arrow from 0 to 4, saying as you do so: We start at 0 and count spaces, one, two, three, four. Then, as the students count the four crosses, draw a second curved arrow beginning at four, saying as you do so: We start at 4 and count the spaces, one, two, three, four. The second arrow will end at the numeral 8 as shown on this number line.

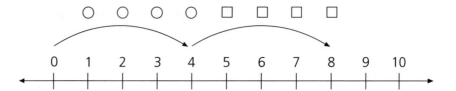

Say: Let's see how many objects we have altogether. Draw a third arrow underneath the number line starting at 0 and ending at 8. Finally, ask one of the students to write the number sentence to show what you have done. The diagram will now looked like this:

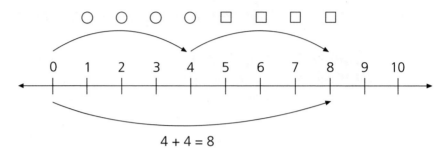

$$4 + 4 = 8$$

Erase the circles, the squares and arrows, but leave the number line and the number sentence on the board. Say: We can draw the arrows for this number sentence. Help one of the students to repeat the procedure for drawing the arrows, remembering that from this point onwards the students will be working directly on the number line without reference to any circles or squares on the board.

Let the students draw arrows to represent other number sentences, for example:
$$2 + 2 = 4$$
$$2 + 3 = 5$$

Then write an incomplete number sentence on the board, for example:
$$2 + 4 = \underline{\quad}$$

This time the students should use the arrows to find the answer to the problem and complete the number sentence. Repeat with similar incomplete number sentences.

Draw another number line on the board and number it from zero to ten. Begin this lesson by repeating some examples from the previous one.

Next, put a set of six large objects on your desk where everyone can see them. Take away one from the set. Ask:
- What number sentence shows what I have done? ($6 - 1 = 5$.)
- Do we get more or less when we take away? (Less.)

Explain that you can show this on the number line. Put the six objects together again. Ask:
- How many objects do I have? (Six.)
- How can I show this on the number line? (Start at 0 and count on to 6.)

Pick up one of the six objects and ask:
- How many do I take away? (One.)
- Do I have more or less objects left? (Less.)

- How can you show that on the number line? (Count back.)
- Why do you count back? (Because when you add, you count on and get more, so now that you are taking away, you must count back to get less.)

Say: Start at six and count back one. Where are you now? (At five.) The number line should look like this:

Repeat using two or three similar examples.

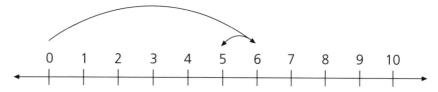

Turn to page 42. Instruct the students to complete the sums using the number line. If they get confused by doing more than one sum on the same number line, you can get them to use different colour pencils or you can reproduce the number line sheet from page 20 of this Teacher's Guide.

Play the following game in the playground. Prepare a box with number cards showing numerals from 1 to 20. Select 20 students, and ask them to each select a number card. Tell them that when you clap your hands they must line up in order. Play until all the students have had a chance.

Unit 39 Sum patterns

Pupil Book page 43

Materials
- sets of 20 objects for groups of students to use

Objectives

Students should be able to:

 demonstrate relationships among number facts for addition and subtraction

Suggested approach

Write the following number sentences on the board:

4 + 5 = 9	9 − 5 = 4
5 + 4 = 9	9 − 4 = 5

Ask the students if they notice anything about these number sentences. (They contain the same three numbers.) Tell the students that addition and subtraction are the opposite of each other.

Use a number line, or small objects, to demonstrate the relationships between these number facts.

Organise the students into groups and give each group 20 objects. Ask the learners to make each of the number sentences on the board using their objects. Check that each group is doing this correctly.

Ask one group to make up a number sentence, for example 3 + 6 = 9. On the board write:

6 ... 3 ... 9
9 ... 6 ... 3
9 ... 3 ... 6

Ask a student to come to the board and fill in the missing signs.

Repeat using different number sentences, this time asking the students to fill in some numbers and signs.

Instruct students to complete page 43 in Pupil Book A.

Unit 40   Longer or shorter?

Pupil Book page 44

Materials
- strips of paper of different lengths and colours
- paste, tape
- other objects of different lengths to compare (string, pencils, Pupil Books); have some equal in length

Objectives
Students should be able to:

 use the terms 'longer than', 'shorter than' and 'equal to'

 estimate and compare lengths sensibly.

Suggested approach

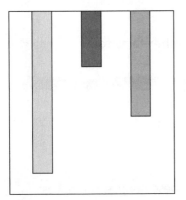

Draw a horizontal line on the board and stick three coloured strips of paper to it so that one end of each touches the line and the other end hangs down to different lengths.

Ask the students questions about the number of strips and their colours. For example: Which strip is the longest? How many strips are there? Compare the lengths of the three strips – which are longer, shorter?

Give one student a strip of paper and say: Find a strip that is longer than the one you have. Let the student show why the strip is longer and let the class decide whether the answer is correct. Repeat this using shorter and equal lengths.

Divide the class into small groups. Give each group about 20 strips of 15 cm ¥ 2cm paper and some paste. Show the class how to use the strips to make a paper chain.

Instruct each group to make two paper chains of different lengths, none using more than twelve links.

Let the students compare the lengths of the chains made by each group. One group should show their chains and other groups should show their chains that are longer than, shorter than or equal in length to the ones shown. Ask the students to show how they decided on their answers (by counting, matching or measuring).

Allow the students to arrange strips of paper and pencils in order of length from shortest to longest. Let them say who has the longest pencil, shortest pencil, and so on.

Introduce the Pupil Book activity on page 44. You may need to read the instructions to make sure that the students know they are circling the longest object in 1 and the shortest object in 2. Have them draw a longer worm in 3.

When the students have completed the Pupil Book page, let them stand and recite the number verse One two buckle my shoe. Let them clap twelve times and then jump twelve times while they count.

Ask the students to look at things that are short or long on the way home and be prepared to tell about these things in the next lesson.

Unit 41 Looking back

Pupil Book page 45

Objectives

Students should be able to:

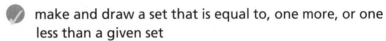 make and draw a set that is equal to, one more, or one less than a given set

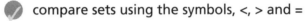 compare sets using the symbols, <, > and =

 add two one-digit numbers.

Suggested approach

This is a review lesson, which covers the skills and knowledge taught in the preceding units.

Read the instructions to the class. Let the students attempt the questions. Give guidance only as necessary. When the students have completed the Pupil Book page, discuss each of the questions and answers with them.

Note which students have difficulty and reinforce or reteach concepts as necessary.

Unit 42 How much have you learned?

Pupil Book page 46

Objectives

Students should be able to:

- select and use their own criteria to classify two-dimensional shapes
- add two one-digit numbers using objects and pictures/diagrams
- subtract a one-digit number using objects and pictures/diagrams.

Suggested approach

This is an assessment lesson in which the students are tested on the concepts taught in the previous units.

Read the instructions to the class, so they all know what they have to do. When the students have completed the Pupil Book page, discuss each of the questions and answers with them.

Note which students have difficulty. You may want to give these students extra practice with these concepts.

Unit 43 Numbers to 10

Pupil Book page 47

Materials

- large number cards showing numerals 1 to 10
- sheets of paper with one to ten objects shown on them
- scrap paper for drawing
- numeral cards from 1 to 10 for each student

Objectives

Students should be able to:

- count from zero to ten
- write the numerals from 0 to 10
- complete and say the words for numbers from zero to ten.

Suggested approach

Give each student a set of number cards and a sheet of paper to draw on. Pin up the picture of one object. Ask the students how many objects this shows. (One.) Hold up the large numeral card showing 1 and pin it to the left of the picture. Let the students find their own number card showing 1.

Stand with your back to the class and trace over the numeral 1 pinned to the board. Tell the class to copy your action using their own numeral card.

Draw the numeral 1 on the board and help students to copy it onto their sheets of paper. Let them practise it.

Teach the rest of the numerals and their words in the same way.

Turn to page 47. Read the instructions to the students but allow them to complete the activity independently. Check their work when they are done to make sure that they are able to form numerals properly and to match numerals to number words and amounts.

When they have completed the page, let them recite their number verses and count to 10 using objects that are available in the classroom.

Units 44 to 47 Working with numbers to 20

Pupil Book pages 48 to 51

Materials
- counters or bottle-caps
- scrap paper

Objectives

Students should be able to:

 read and write numbers up to twenty in words and numerals

 count and identify the number of objects in a set of up to twenty objects

 make and draw sets of up to twenty objects.

Suggested approach

Draw eleven objects on the board. Ask a student to count the objects and tell the rest of the class how many objects there are.

Ask another student to draw a circle around ten of them. Ask: How many tens are there? (One.) How many are left over? (One.)

Show how the number of objects drawn can be recorded as:
$10 + 1 = 11$

The students can use the bottle-caps to represent this number sum. Ask them to practise writing the sum on their pieces of scrap paper.

Add one more object to the ones you have drawn on the board. Ask the students how this could be recorded. They should suggest $10 + 2 = 12$.

Repeat this procedure to 20 by adding one object each time and getting the students to record as previously.

Give the students numbers in the form shown below and ask them to set out bottle-caps to represent them:
$10 + 8 = 18$ $10 + 6 = 16$

Practise counting with the students from 0 to 20.

Instruct the students to complete pages 48 to 51 in Pupil Book A. You may want them to do each unit as you complete the relevant numbers.

Unit 48 Numbers to 20

Pupil Book page 52

Objectives

Students should be able to:

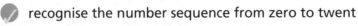 recognise the number sequence from zero to twent

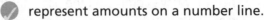 represent amounts on a number line.

Suggested approach

Turn to page 52. The first activity requires the students to fill in the missing numbers on the number lines. The second activity requires them to draw lines to join the number symbols in the shapes to the correct points on the number line. Let the students complete the number sequences by writing the missing numerals. Let them join the dots and colour the pictures.

Unit 49 Number order

Pupil Book page 53

Objectives

Students should be able to:

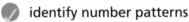 identify number patterns

sequence numbers to 20.

Suggested approach

The students should be able to complete this page with little or no support. Use it to reinforce previously taught concepts and as an opportunity to assist students who had difficulty with these concepts before.

Unit 50 Number names and sentences

Pupil Book page 54

Materials
- twelve bottle-caps per student
- a set of cards with symbols, names or pictures as shown for numbers to 20

Objectives

Students should be able to:

use number names and write number sentences.

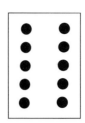

Write the number names from one to twenty on the board. Then write the number symbols from 1 to 20 in any order and ask several students to match the names and symbols.

Divide the class into three teams, A, B and C. Give all the students in team A the cards with number symbols, give the students in team B the cards with number names, and give the students in team C the cards with pictures. Then play this game with the class. Call out a number. The first person to identify it by symbol, name or picture gets a point for their team.

Ask the students to put three bottle-caps on the desk. Then ask them to put out four more. Ask how many there are in all. Question the students to come up with the correct number sentences: $3 + 4 = 7$.

Turn to page 54. Discuss each activity with the class and let them tell you what should be done. Allow them to complete the activities independently, observing them as they work to identify any problems and to praise those who are doing well.

Unit 51   Equal, one more, one less

Pupil Book page 55

Objectives

Students should be able to:

 make and draw a set that is equal to, one more than or one less than a given set.

Put fifteen counters in a row on a desk. Ask a student to make another row that has an equal number of counters.

Ask another student to make a row with one less, beside the row of fifteen counters. Ask another student to count the counters in each of the two rows. Let the students continue making rows until there is only one counter in a row. Let a student count each new set as it is made.

By adding an extra can to the second row and taking it away again, show that the second row is the same as the first with one can taken away, that is, with one less. Demonstrate that the same is true for the other rows.

Repeat the procedure, but this time start with one counter and ask students to add one counter to each row. They should count the number of counters in each row that they make. Continue until there are twenty counters in a row.

Instruct students to complete page 55 of Pupil Book A.

Unit 52   My weather graph

Pupil Book page 56

Materials
- large block graph for display
- coloured squares to stick onto graph

Objectives

Students should be able to:

 present information on a bar graph.

Suggested approach

Have the students turn to page 56. Read the symbols with the class and make sure they know that each symbol represents a specific type of weather. Ask the students to write the date in their books. Under that, have them draw a symbol to show the weather today.

Explain that Andrew has drawn a graph to show the weather each day for a week. Read the names of the days with the class. As you read, let the students say what kind of weather was recorded on that day. For example, Monday – the sun was shining.

Allow the students to answer the questions on their own. Check to see that they have three days of sun and two days of rain.

Record the weather for a week.

Remember to come back to this chart next week to check it. You could also prepare a large chart for the classroom so that students can compare their graphs with the one on display.

Unit 53   Numbers around us

Pupil Book page 57

Materials
- examples of numbers in real life

Objectives

Students should be able to:

 find numbers around them

 write the numerals 1 to 5.

Suggested approach

Play some number games and sing some of the number songs before using this page.

Turn to page 57. Look at the photographs. They show numbers on a telephone, numbers on the jerseys of football players, numbers on a car number plate, numbers on the dial of a stove. Ask the children to say the numbers aloud and let them guess what the photographs show before you tell them. Ask them to say where else they would find numbers around them. Let them choose one example and draw it.

The 'talk about' box on page 57 asks the students to think about numbers in the environment. Encourage them to give as many examples as possible. Answers might include: dates on newspapers, page numbers, money, addresses, postal codes, amounts on packages, prices, model numbers of appliances or cars, times, timetables, phone numbers, and so on. Show the class the examples that you have found. It might not be possible to say how many numbers we use in a day exactly, but lead the students to the realisation that there are many, many numbers around us.

Let the students practise writing the numerals 1 to 5 by filling them in on the clock face and on the calculator keys.

Units 54 and 55   Mass

Pupil Book pages 58 and 59

Materials

- various objects for weighing (see activities) including a big paper bag full of leaves or crumpled paper and a smaller but heavier bag of sand
- objects that could be considered heavy
- a balance scale

Objectives

Students should be able to:

 classify objects as heavy or light

 use a balance scale to measure and compare mass.

Suggested approach

Place the objects on the table. Let different students in turn come to the front of the class and say whether they think they can lift the objects. Let them try to lift or move some of them. Ask questions such as the following:

- Which object was hard to pick up?
- Which object was easy to pick up?
- Was the football easier to pick up than the table tennis ball?
- Why do you think the brick was not easy to move?
- Could you lift the brick with one hand?

The students' answers may relate to the materials from which the object is made, the purpose that it serves, the size of the object, and so on. Acknowledge all answers and then explain that these features can cause an object to be heavy or light.

Draw two large circles on the floor and label them A and B. Let some students come in turn and place the heavy objects in circle A and the light objects in circle B. If anyone finds it difficult to lift an object, let them say in which circle it should be placed, then allow another student to help them carry it. The other students should say whether the object is correctly placed each time.

Turn to page 58. Discuss the drawings so that the students know what is shown in each picture. Read the instructions to the class and let them complete the colouring activity.

Pass around two objects, one of which is considerably heavier than the other. Let the students hold one in each hand and tell what happens. They should be able to explain that one hand is pushed downwards. When they tell you, find out if they know the words 'heavier' and 'lighter'. Develop the idea by asking questions that prompt the class to reply by saying such things as:

- This chair is heavier than that book.
- John (choose the biggest boy in the class) is heavier than Jane (the smallest girl).
- That pencil is lighter than this ruler.

Continue until they come to two objects that they are unsure about, for example, two bananas of about the same size. Say: Let's see how we can tell which is heavier.

Display the balance scale and take the two objects which the class are sure about (for example a pencil and a lime). Put one of the objects on one scale pan and one on the other and ask the class to tell you what happens. (The pan with the heavier object on it goes down.) Say: Let's see if this always happens.

Take the objects off the pans, then put them back again, and ask: Did the pan with the heavier object go down? (Yes.) Take the objects off the pans, and reverse them, putting them on opposite sides from before. Ask again: Did the pan with the heavier object go down? (Yes.) Repeat this with other pairs of objects that the class are sure about, for example a matchbox full of sand and an empty matchbox. Before putting the objects on the pans ask the students to predict what will happen and then to watch closely. Ask each time: Were you right? The fact that the pan with the heavier object on it always goes down is not something that all children easily grasp.

Pick up the two objects the class were unsure about, and ask: How can we tell for sure which is heavier? (Put them on the pans and see which pan goes down.) Demonstrate while the class watches carefully. Let them say what happens and tell you which object is heavier. Take the objects off the pans, prepare to reverse them on the pans, and ask them to say what will happen. Let them see if they are right.

Turn to page 59. Ask the students to say which object is heavier on each balance scale. Let them colour the heavier object in each pair. Discuss the pairs of objects shown at the bottom of the page. Read the instructions to the class and let them complete the activities independently.

Unit 56 Are they the same?

Pupil Book page 60

Materials
- small objects to use to demonstrate the sets

Objectives

Students should be able to:

 apply the commutative law to simple addition sums.

Suggested approach

Demonstrate equal and unequal sets using concrete examples. Teach the students that an equals sign with a stroke through it means 'not equal to' (≠). As you demonstrate, have the students give number sentences for what you are showing, for example, $2 + 3 \neq 4 + 2$.

Let the students use real objects to model two sets. Teach them to say the addition from left to right and then from right to left. When you are confident that they can do this have them complete section 2 on page 60.

Use section 3 to reinforce bonds and the commutative law. Instruct the students to work from top to bottom so that they complete the first column before moving on to the second column.

 Additional activities

For additional practice with the commutative law, give the students the following table.
They must draw lines to connect the matching sums.

Column 1	Column 2
3 + 4	2 + 4
2 + 1	3 + 2
8 + 2	3 + 15
4 + 12	1 + 2
15 + 3	4 + 3
2 + 3	2 + 8

You can fill in more examples on a similar table if you want to give students further practice.

Unit 57   Adding one

Pupil Book page 61

Materials
- large number symbol cards
- clothesline and pegs

Objectives
Students should be able to:

 recognise the number sequence from zero to ten

 skip count on a number line to add one.

Suggested approach

Place the number cards on a desk. Let two students hold up the clothesline in front of the class. Explain to the class that they are going to put the numbers on a number line. Ask someone to peg the card showing zero on the clothesline. Then ask another student to find the card that comes after zero, and peg it beside the first. Repeat this procedure with each card up to ten. Emphasise the sequence of the cards by asking questions, for example: Which number comes after three? (Four.)

Take the numbers off the line, and then repeat the procedure, this time starting at ten and working downwards. Emphasise the use of the word 'before', for example: What number comes before ten? ... Before one?

Beginning again with the empty line, call on individual students to peg the following numbers on the number line: 0, 1, 3, 5, 7, 9. Ask other students to peg the missing numbers in their correct places. For example, say: Come out and peg up the card that has seven on it. Now peg up the card that has nine on it. What number comes between them? (Eight.) Let the student who gave the answer peg that card in the proper place.

Turn to page 61. Show the students how to use a finger to make jumps on the number line. Start at any number, for example, two. Tell the class to put their fingers on the two. Ask them: What number is one more than two? (Three.) Demonstrate, making a jump to show one more. Let the students complete the rest of the activity on their own. Make sure that they can use the number line as it forms the basis of future skip counting lessons.

Unit 58   Combining sets

Pupil Book page 62

Objectives
Students should be able to:

 perform simple addition sums.

By now, the students should be ready to do the activities on their own. Help them to find the correct page and read the instruction if necessary but otherwise let them work independently. Go around the class helping those students who need individual attention and praising all efforts.

Units 59 and 60   Cents

Pupil Book pages 63 and 64

Materials

- small denomination coins
- cardboard coin facsimiles for each student
- number symbol cards
- bottle of sweets
- paper bag

Objectives

Students should be able to:

 recognise the one-cent, five-cent, $1 and $5 coins

 add small coin amounts

add money amounts up to five cents.

Suggested approach

Note: We have tried to provide a generic lesson outline for dealing with money. However, you will need to adapt all money lessons to suit the currency used in your territory.

Ask questions that will draw upon the students' experience with coins. For example:

- What are some of the things you like to buy at the shop or at school?
- Have you been to the shop?
- Have you been to the market?
- What are some of the things you buy there?
- What do you give in exchange for the things you buy?

Then ask the students to name some coins. They may name the five-cent coin, the ten-cent coin, and so on. Distribute the real coins to the students and let them talk about them. Ask questions such as: What do you notice about the colour, size, shape, weight and edges of the coins?

Draw pictures of coins on the board and tell the children what they are. Name each coin again and put the numeral underneath each one as you name it. For example: This is the one-cent coin. (Put the numeral 1 underneath it.) This is the five-cent coin. (Put the numeral 5 underneath it.) Do the same for the dollar coins.

Say the name of a coin. Have the students pick up the matching coin and show it to you. Put the coins in line on the desk. Go round the class making sure the students have put their coins in the proper sequence.

Sometime during the day, when the students have completed the Pupil Book pages, arrange the class in groups of five children. Give each group 20 one-cent coins. The groups are to count the money, for example, one cent, two cents, three cents, and so on. Each member of the group should be given the opportunity to count the coins.

Turn to page 63. Look at the coins in the photograph. These are one-cent coins from Barbados and Trinidad and Tobago. See which coins the students can recognise.

The 'talk about' box requires the students to read the names on the coins. Allow them to talk about their knowledge of Barbados and Trinidad and Tobago. Let the class see how many Caribbean countries they can name. If you like you can make a list of the names on the board or on a poster to display in the classroom.

Have the students complete the activity on page 63 by colouring in the correct number of one-cent coins. Check to see that they are all able to do this. Allow students who struggle to use real coins to model answers.

Put a set of different coins in a paper bag. Ask two students to come to the front of the class. Say: We are going to play a game. Peter, you take this bag. Shake it a little, and tell Mary which coin you want her to take out of the bag. Mary will feel in the bag and select the coin without looking. Check to see that Mary is right. The other students may also check the selection. Repeat with other pairs of students. Allow them to choose their own partners.

Turn to page 64. Explain to the class that they are going to draw the coins that they need to pay for each amount. They can use small circular shapes or objects as templates for the coins. They could also use real coins to draw around. Walk around as they are working to make sure they can do this. Help those children who need assistance.

Additional activities

Prepare play coins and a bottle of one cent 'sweets' for the class shop. Introduce the class to the shop and let the students talk about some of the items. Ask two students to come and stand facing the class. Give each of them a coin and say what it is, for example, one cent, five cents.

Ask the students questions about the coins. Let each hold their coin up as they speak. Ask: Which is the largest in size? Which is the smallest? Which is the lightest? Ask the children to name the coin that they have. Then ask: What is the colour of the one-cent piece?

Take a bottle of sweets from the class shop and say: The sweets cost one cent each. Ask: Which coin buys more sweets? Which coin buys fewer sweets? How can you tell? Let other students 'sell' the sweets.

This procedure will help the class to think of the different properties of coins and realise that the coin that is bigger in size does not necessarily buy more sweets.

Unit 61 Squares and rectangles

Pupil Book page 65

Objectives
Students should be able to:

 name and recognise basic 2D shapes

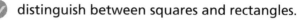 distinguish between squares and rectangles.

Suggested approach

Unit 61 is an important unit; it revises and reinforces the concept of square and rectangle. It is important for students to learn that a square is a type of rectangle, but a rectangle is not a square. Ensure that the students discuss this both among themselves and with you. Try to allow them to discover the differences themselves.

After discussion, turn to page 65, and have the students point out all the squares. Let them work co-operatively to do this and to check each other's responses. Once you and they are sure they have identified all the squares correctly, let them colour the squares blue. Repeat this with the rectangles.

Unit 62 Looking back

Pupil Book page 66

Objectives
Students should be able to:

 identify and name rectangles and squares

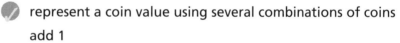 represent a coin value using several combinations of coins add 1

  read and write numbers up to twenty in numerals and words

  compare the mass of two objects.

Suggested approach

This is a review lesson, which covers the skills and knowledge taught in the preceding units.

Read the instructions to the class. Let the students attempt the questions. Give guidance only as necessary. When the students have completed the Pupil Book page, discuss each of the questions and answers with them.

Note which students have difficulty and reinforce or reteach concepts as necessary.

Unit 63 How much have you learned?

Pupil Book page 67

> ### Objectives
> Students should be able to:
> - compare the mass of two objects
> - make and draw a set that is equal to, one more or one less than a given set
> - compare sets using the symbols <, > and =
> - identify rectangles
> - read and write numbers up to twenty in numerals and words.

Suggested approach

This is an assessment lesson in which the students are tested on the concepts taught in the previous units.

Read the instructions to the class, so they all know what they have to do. When the students have completed the Pupil Book page, discuss each of the questions and answers with them.

Note which students have difficulty. You may want to give these students extra practice with these concepts.

Unit 64 Comparing sets

Pupil Book page 68

Materials
- number line tape with number symbol cards one to 20

> ### Objectives
> Students should be able to:
> - compare the size of sets using the number line
> - use the symbols <, > and =.

Suggested approach

Let a student come forward and hold a number line tape so that everyone can see it. Ask a set of six girls to stand behind the tape and to give themselves numbers using the number symbol cards 1 to 6. Then ask four boys to stand in front of the tape and give themselves numbers using the cards 1 to 4.

Ask:
- Are there more girls or more boys? (More girls.)
- How many more? (Two more.)
- How many girls in all? (Six.)
- How many boys? (Four.)
- How many more girls than boys? (Two more.)

Unit-by-unit support for Pupil Book 1A Unit 63; Unit 64

Say: Yes, six is more than four. How can we write that as a number sentence? (6 > 4.)

Repeat with other groups of students, using different sets of numbers. Use equal sets as well.

Draw a number line from one to ten on the board and put a set of eight crosses above the line. Students should come forward and draw lines from the crosses to the numerals on the number line until the drawing looks like this:

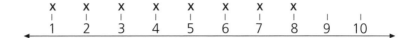

Now draw five circles below the line and let the students match them as before. The diagram should look something like this:

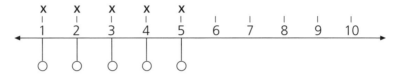

Ask:
- Which set is greater? (The crosses.)
- How many more crosses than circles? (Three more.)
- How do we write the number sentence that shows eight is more than five? (8 > 5.)

Repeat with other sets, using equal sets as well as smaller sets.

Turn to page 68. For activities 1 and 2, let the students draw lines from the objects of one set to the correct numeral on the number line, and again from the objects of the second set to the correct numeral on the number line. They should then complete the number sentences below each example. In activity 3, the students can draw their own diagrams and number lines if necessary to complete the number sentences.

CD-Rom activity
- <, > or =

Units 65 to 69   Working with numbers to 19

Pupil Book pages 69 to 73

Materials
- counters or bottle-caps

Objectives

Students should be able to:
- recognise and use numbers from 10 to 19
- break down numbers into tens and units
- combine sets of tens and units to make amounts to 19.

tens	ones
1	1

$10 + 2 = 12$

Draw eleven objects on the board as shown on the left.

Ask a student to count the objects, and ask another student to draw a circle round ten of them. Ask: How many tens are there? (One.) How many are left over? (One.) Draw columns on the board as shown on the left.

Show how the number of objects drawn can be recorded as: $10 + 1 = 11$.

Add one more object. Ask the students how this could be recorded. They should suggest: $10 + 2 = 12$.

Repeat this procedure to 19, by adding one object each time and getting the students to record as previously. Explain that we do not usually write 'tens' and 'ones' each time and must remember that, say, 15 is one ten and five ones.

Give the students numbers in the form shown below and ask them to set out counters to represent them:
$10 + 8 = 18$ $10 + 6 = 16$

Repeat this for numbers without the 'tens' and 'ones', for example 19, 15.

Turn to page 69. Let the students complete the activities without giving them further help. They can use the examples at the top of the page for guidance.

tens	ones
1	5

Draw 15 objects on the board. Ask a student to draw a circle around ten of them. Ask another student to say how many are left outside the circle. (Five.) Show how this can be written as 15, using the same method described in previous steps.

Let the students set out 17 counters and put ten of them together. Ask how many are left. (Seven.) The students should then record this as 17. Repeat with all the other numbers from 11 to 19. Encourage the students to read out these numbers to ensure that they know the number names.

Turn to page 70. The students draw a circle around ten objects, then count the remaining ones. Then they record the amounts in a number sentence. The students should read out some of their answers.

Turn to page 71. Give the students counters to use to model the sums. Show them how to make a group of ten and four loose objects. Have them count the total and complete the number sentences. Have them complete the rest of activity on their own. Walk around and assist the students who are struggling.

Turn to page 72. The sets in these examples look different and students are expected to apply their knowledge of the relationship between addition and subtraction in order to complete the activity. Complete the first example with the class. Show them how to count the number of shapes in the total and if necessary let them cover up those shown on the left. Teach them to count the left-over shapes and then draw the same amount to make the missing sets. When they can do this they should complete the number sentences.

Ask the students to make two sets of nine counters. Write 9 + 9 on the board. Ask the students to count how many counters they have. Ask a student to come to the board and complete the number sentence by writing in the correct answer.

Repeat with different number sentences with totals up to 20. Ask the student to try and work out the answers without using counters if they can.

Arrange the students in pairs. Ask each of them to create two number sentences for their partner to solve (the totals must be 20 or less). Observe the students as they work to make sure that they can create and solve these problems.

CD-Rom activity
■ Addition (to 19)

Use page 73 to have students draw and practise simple bonds to 19. Check the completed work to see which students can manage these. Observe students as they work to see who is becoming less reliant on counters and who still needs to work with concrete apparatus.

Unit 70   Matchstick shapes

Pupil Book page 74

Materials
■ spent matches

Objectives

Students should be able to:

name and recognise basic 2D shapes

Suggested approach

Unit 70 follows on from recognising and making pictures with shapes to constructing your own shapes. This allows the students to begin to understand the concept of polygons. Give each group of students a pile of spent matches. Before you do anything with the matches, discuss the 'talk about' box. Point out that it is extremely dangerous to play with unspent matches. For those territories following an integrated curriculum, this is an ideal time to discuss safety in the home.

Look at the matchstick shapes on page 74. Ask individual students to describe the shapes, have them name the shape and say how many matches we used to build it. Note that the matches in the photograph are plastic and thus look unspent. Give the groups some time to make the shapes shown. Walk around and check that each group has managed to make all four shapes.

Ask the students to take four matches and make a shape with them. It is likely they will make a square. Check the shapes and then instruct the students to draw the shape next to the four matches. Repeat this with six matches.

Units 71 to 73 Measuring

Pupil Book pages 75 to 77

Materials
- paper strips from earlier lesson
- matchboxes
- coloured elbow macaroni and string

Objectives
Students should be able to:

 use the concepts of longer than, shorter than and equal lengths

 begin to estimate lengths.

Suggested approach

Revise the words 'long' and 'short' by asking students to talk about what they saw yesterday on their way home from school in terms of lengths. They may say things like: On my way home I saw a dog with a long tail. I have a long skipping rope. My father has short hair.

Draw a horizontal line on the board and stick several pairs of paper strips beneath it. Ask students which strip in each pair is longer. Ask other students to say which strip is shorter.

Introduce the concept 'taller than' by having two students of different heights stand in front of the class. Ask the students: Who is taller/ shorter? Encourage the students to use the words taller and shorter in describing the two students. (John is shorter than Charles, and so on.) Encourage them to express their observation using the expressions 'shorter than' and 'taller than'.

Ask one students to make a stack of matchboxes on the desk. Then ask another student to make a stack that is taller and another student to make one that is not as tall.

Stand facing the class with a strip of paper in each hand. Ask: Which is longer? When the class has told you which strip they believe is longer, ask: How can we find out which is longer? (Put them together and match them.)

Match the strips in this way to show students whether they were right or wrong. Repeat a few times, and then hold a strip of paper in each hand. Ask: Which is shorter? When the students have told you which strip they believe is shorter, ask: How can we find out which is shorter? (Put them together and match them.)

Take students on the nature walk and instruct them to identify objects that are longer, shorter or taller than some other objects they have seen. Encourage them to talk about what they have seen, for example, 'the breadfruit tree is taller than the mango tree.'

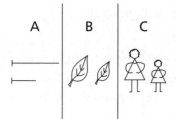

Draw three columns on the board and draw objects as shown on the left. Draw attention to the three columns, A, B and C. Let a student come forward and ask them to mark or tick the longer object in column A. Ask another student to mark the shorter object in column B, and a third to mark the taller object in column C. When the students have understood the idea let them complete page 75.

Refer to the additional activities at the end of this unit. Then turn to page 76. Explain to the students that they are going to colour one object in each set. Read the instructions with the class. This gives valuable practice in reading words such as 'length', 'longer' and 'shorter'. Allow them to complete activity and check each other's work.

Turn to page 77. There are 15 activities to do on this page. Make sure that the students know they are to colour one object in each set. In the first column they are to colour the shorter object. In the second column they are to colour the longer object in each pair. In the third column they are to colour the taller object in each pair. Have the class colour one object in each column to make sure that they are doing the right thing. Walk around and check their work. Help those children who need it.

Additional activities

Unit 72 provides a good opportunity to work with patterns. Provide coloured elbow macaroni in a range of colours. Give each student a piece of string and have them thread it through the macaroni to make necklaces and bracelets of different lengths. Encourage them to use specified and unspecified patterns. Allow them to compare the lengths of their necklaces and bracelets before they complete Unit 72.

Unit 74 Counting cents

Pupil Book page 78

Materials
- small objects for each student to use as counters
- one-cent coins for counting

Objectives
Students should be able to:

 find the total value of a combination of coins

 combine smaller sets to make sets with up to nine objects.

Suggested approach

Give each student a number of one-cent coins to use as counters. Tell the students to make a set of four objects on one side of the desk and a set of one object on the other side. When you say 'Go', they should push the objects across the desk to join the sets. Ask: What did you do? (Put the two sets together.) Ask: How many do you have now? (Five.) Say: Yes, four and one make five. Write the number sentence on the board:
4 + 1 = 5.

Repeat with other examples, extending the number range up to nine. Once you are sure that the students can do this using concrete materials, let them work through Pupil Book page 78.

Unit 75 Measuring containers

Pupil Book page 79

Materials
- a sink or basin
- water and sand
- containers of various sizes
- flashcards with 'full', 'holds more', 'holds less', 'spoonfuls'

Objectives
Students should be able to:

 estimate the amount that a container can hold using informal units

 measure in informal units to check estimates.

Suggested approach

It is important for students to have plenty of experience of measuring in practical situations. In this unit they will work with containers that have different volumes. Practical activities for teaching volume include working with water and working with sand.

When working with water, use a sink or a large basin full of water, and work outside to avoid mess. Invite the students to estimate which of two containers holds more. They can find out by pouring from one container to the other. Emphasise that they should pour water carefully, trying not to spill. They should also consider when a container is full. Put the flashcard saying 'holds more' next to the container that holds more. A wide variety of shapes and sizes of container should be provided and the activity should be repeated several times.

Invite the students to estimate, for example, how many cups of water fill a dish. They could then find out by filling and counting the number of cups of water required. Again, encourage them to work carefully and not to spill water when pouring from the cup into the dish. Note that the answer will not be an exact number of cups and might vary slightly from one student to another.

When working with sand, use a large tray or shallow bath containing sand. Use cardboard cartons and boxes. Ask the students to estimate which of two containers holds more. They can then find out by filling one container with sand and pouring it into the other. Put the flashcard with the words 'holds more' next to the container that holds more. Ask the students to estimate, for example, how many spoonfuls of sand will fill the cup. They can then find out by counting how many spoonfuls are required. The word 'spoonfuls' should be taught by using a flashcard.

Turn to page 79. This page requires the students to compare the volume of two containers, first by estimating, then by measuring and counting to check the estimates. Work through the first example with the class. Ask questions such as: Does a hand or a bowl hold more? What do you think? Have the students write 'hand' or 'bowl' next to 'Guess'. Next, let them use sand or water with a hand and a bowl to check. Let them write 'hand' or 'bowl' next to 'Measure'.

Unit-by-unit support for Pupil Book 1A Unit 75

Unit 76 Full and empty

Pupil Book page 80

Materials
- different sizes of containers
- sand and/or water
- a plastic one litre bottle and a 250 ml plastic cup for each group

Objectives

Students should be able to:

 understand and use the terms 'full' and 'empty'.

Suggested approach

Before you tackle the material in the Pupil Book you need to have a practical lesson using as many different types and sizes of containers as possible. Working outside, give the students various tasks to get them familiar with the concepts of full, empty, half-full. For example, you could give them containers or bottles of the following capacities: 125 ml, 250 ml, 500 ml, 750 ml, 1 _, 1_ _. Show the class an empty 250 ml container. Ask: Is empty or full? (Empty.) Then fill the container with water. Ask again: Is it empty or full? (Full.) Show a 500 ml bottle. Ask: Do you think this one holds more or less water than the smaller one? (More.) Is it empty or full? (Empty.) I'm going to pour the water from the smaller container into this one. Do you think it will fill this bottle? (No.) How many times do you think I must pour the amount from the smaller bottle into the bigger bottle to make it full? (Twice.)

Continue in the same way. Emphasise the concepts full, half-full, or empty.

Once you are satisfied that the students know the difference between full, empty, half-empty and half-full, turn to Pupil Book page 80. Let the students complete the colouring activity on their own. Once they are finished, ask questions such as: How many full containers are there? (Three.) And so on.

Unit 77 Whole and half

Pupil Book page 81

Materials
- square, rectangular and circular cards

Objectives

Students should be able to:

 understand the concept of a fraction.

Suggested approach

Give each student a square, circular or rectangular card. Fold your shape in half and the tear the shape in half.

Ask the students what they would call the piece that I have torn off this shape. Tell them you have torn the shape into two parts that are the same. You can show them this by laying one piece on top of the other. The students should be able to see that the two parts are the same.

Tell them that you have torn the shape in half. There are two halves in every whole.

Repeat the activity using different shapes.

Instruct the students to complete page 81 of Pupil Book A.

Unit 78   Folding paper

Pupil Book page 82

Materials
- paper
- scissors
- cans or round objects

Objectives
Students should be able to:
 cut and fold simple shapes to find a line of symmetry
 begin to explore simple halves.

Suggested approach

Turn to page 82. Ask the students what they can see in the photographs. Give each student two pieces of paper and a pair of scissors. Instruct them to keep one piece of paper rectangular. Give them cans or other round objects and have them draw a circle on the second piece of paper. Then cut out the circles. If the students are unable to do this you might like to supply them with circles instead. Ask the students to fold both pieces of paper in half. Demonstrate this if necessary. Once they have folded them in half, have them colour one half only.

The 'talk about' box asks the students to talk about what they notice. Allow them to share their ideas with the class before moving on. Ensure that they realise that they have coloured one half of the shape and that the other half is the same shape as the one they have coloured.

In activity 2, the students are expected to colour one half of each shape. It is not necessary that they use the terms 'half' or 'symmetry' at this stage. Simply read the instructions and let the students complete the activity on their own. Check to see that they have managed to complete the activity.

Units 79 and 80   Half of a set

Pupil Book pages 83 and 84

Materials
- twelve bottle-caps for each pair of students

Objectives
Students should be able to:
 find half of a set of objects.

Ask four boys to come out and stand in a line facing the class. Ask a girl to divide the group into halves. She should put two boys in one group into two in the other. Repeat with other even numbers of children: two, six and eight, using both boys and girls. The subgroups need not necessarily be all male or all female. Emphasise that the numbers in each case must be the same in each sub-group.

Let each student find a partner and hand each pair twelve bottle-caps. Indicate clearly the number they are to work with. Say: Now we are going to work with four. Take four bottle-caps and put them on your desk. Take half of the bottle-caps and give your partner the other half. Count and see that both of you have the same number. Repeat with other numbers up to ten. Go around the class checking what the students do.

Turn to page 83. Discuss the example at the top of the page with the class. The two children are sharing a set of four sweets. Each half of the set has been circled. This is the set belonging to each child. If you like, you can join each set to a child by drawing a line. Have the students look at the pictures on the page and ask them how they would share two bones between two dogs. Let them draw the sharing; it does not matter if they include the dog with the set. Let them complete **b** and **c** on their own.

Draw four objects on the board and ask a student to colour half of them. Repeat this with one or two other even amounts. Turn to page 84. Let the students look at the pictures. Explain that they are going to colour half of each set. The students will probably colour clearly symmetrically; in other words, they may colour three on the left and three on the right. However it is equally correct for them to colour in any half. Let the students complete the activities on their own. Walk around and praise them for their efforts.

Pupil Book pages 85 and 86

Materials

- fraction cut-outs
- flannel board
- flashcards with 'yes' and 'no'

Objectives

Students should be able to:

 recognise half of a single object.

Suggested approach

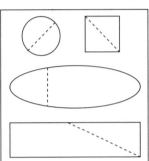

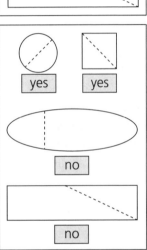

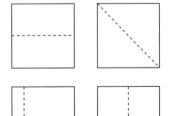

CD-Rom activity
- Whole and half

Place the cut-outs on the flannel board as shown on the left.

Point to the circle and ask: Does this picture show halves? (Yes.) Next, point to the oval and ask: Does this picture show halves? (No.) Why not? (Because the two parts are not the same size.) Ask one of the students to take the circle cut-out from the flannel board and try to find out whether the two parts are the same size. Direct the student to fold the paper along the dashed line. Ask: Are the two pieces the same size? The student may actually need to cut the shape to match the two pieces. Reattach the two equal pieces to the flannel board. Ask again: Does this picture show two halves? (Yes.) Let a student find a 'yes' card and place it below the circle. Repeat the procedure with the other cut-outs. The flannel board should now look like it does on the left.

Remove the 'yes' and 'no' flashcards. Ask individual students to identify on the flannel board all the pictures that show halves. Colour one half of the cut-out in each case.

Teach the class to write the word 'half'.

Turn to page 85. Use the completed example to show the students what they should do. Allow them to complete the activity on their own. Walk around and assist those who need help.

The 'talk about' box involves discussion about equal sharing in real life. Encourage all ideas from the students.

Draw pictures like the ones on the left on the board.

Point to the pictures that you have drawn and ask whether any of them show one half. (Three of them do.) Ask students to come up and write 'half' underneath the pictures that show halves. If there is time, allow them to colour half.

Turn to page 86. Look at the circles in example a. The circle that has been coloured in shows two halves. Have the class write 'half' twice, once on each half. Let the class discuss the other examples in pairs. Allow them to say which of the examples shows half. When they are in agreement, allow them to colour half and write the word 'half' on the separate parts.

Note: You might like to teach the class how to write the symbol $\frac{1}{2}$. If so, demonstrate this on the board and have them write $\frac{1}{2}$ instead of the word in the examples.

Additional activities

You can play games with the students to reinforce the concept of halving. Some examples are given below.

- Have the students sit in a circle, with six students sitting in the middle. Ask half of the six to stand on one leg. Ask the others: How many are standing on one leg? How many are still sitting down? Repeat the game with other numbers and actions.
- Have the students sit in pairs. Give them word problems involving halving. For example: There are eight kittens in a basket. Half of the kittens are ginger and half are black. How many kittens are ginger? Allow different pairs to give answers.

Unit 83 Looking back

Pupil Book page 87

Objectives

Students should be able to:

- use the symbols <, > and = correctly
- identify one-half of a set
- determine the missing number in an addition number sentence
- add single digit numbers to 10
- compare the length of two objects using the words 'longer' and 'shorter'.

Suggested approach

This is a review lesson, which covers the skills and knowledge taught in the preceding units.

Read the instructions to the class. Let the students attempt the questions. Give guidance only as necessary. When the students have completed the Pupil Book page, discuss each of the questions and answers with them.

Note which students have difficulty and reinforce or reteach concepts as necessary.

Pupil Book page 88

Objectives

Students should be able to:

- compare the length of two objects using the words 'longer' and 'shorter'
- identify one-half of a set or an object
- determine the missing number in an addition number sentence
- subtract a one-digit number from numbers up to 20.

Suggested approach

This is an assessment lesson in which the students are tested on the concepts taught in the previous units.

Read the instructions to the class, so they all know what they have to do. When the students have completed the Pupil Book page, discuss each of the questions and answers with them.

Note which students have difficulty. You may want to give these students extra practice with these concepts.

Unit-by-unit support for Pupil Book 1B

Refer to the grid on pages 128 to 132 to see how the curriculum objectives for different territories are covered in this book.

Units 1 and 2   Counting to 50

Pupil Book pages 5 and 6

Materials
- paper bags containing 50 lollipop sticks or spent matches
- five lengths of string
- sheets of cardboard or paper

Objectives
Students should be able to:

 count in sequence to 50.

Suggested approach

Draw a set of ten crosses on the board. Ask the students to count the crosses. Ask: How many tens? (One.) How many ones? (None.) Get the students to write this in a tally chart, and to write the numeral underneath. Do the same with twenty, thirty, forty and fifty, introducing the class to the vocabulary.

Divide the class into groups and give each group a bag containing 50 sticks and five lengths of thread. Let each group begin to make bundles of ten sticks. After a few minutes, stop the activity and ask one of the groups how many bundles of ten it has made. For example, the group may have wrapped three bundles. Ask how many sticks that is (30.) Emphasise that three tens are thirty and so on.

In their groups, ask the students to make a chart containing all the numerals from 1 to 50. Give each group a sheet of card divided into 50 squares (5 × 10). The students should fill in the numerals 1 to 50 in the correct order.

Ask the students to turn to page 5. Ask a volunteer to read out the first ten numbers on the half hundred square. Get another volunteer to read out the next ten numbers. Emphasise that we read from left to right starting with the top row. Ask the students questions about the grid, for example:
- What is one less than 25? … 49? … 27? etc.
- What is one more than 43? … 37? … 19? etc.
- What number is between 48 and 50? … 35 and 37? etc.

Once you feel that the students are comfortable with numbers up to 50, ask them complete pages 5 and 6.

Units 3 to 6 Partitioning sets

Pupil Book pages 7 to 10

Materials
- set of objects for demonstration

Objectives
Students should be able to:

 extend partitioning to include sets of up to 20 objects

 draw missing sets and complete number sentences.

Suggested approach

Turn to page 7. Demonstrate how to partition nine using real objects, using the procedure used previously. Link this to what is shown in the teaching box on page 7. Complete activities 1 and 2 as a class. Note that students will come up with their own different combinations and possibilities.

Review the combination of sets following the procedure used previously. After various combinations have been made, begin to partition sets of nine or more using real objects as before.

Choose a number, for example 14. Ask the class how many ways they think they can partition a set of 14 objects. Let them experiment with bottle-caps and then discuss their answers. Display a chart of the addition facts for 14. Encourage the students to talk about any patterns they see.

0 + 14 = 14	8 + 6 = 14
1 + 13 = 14	9 + 5 = 14
2 + 12 = 14	10 + 4 = 14
3 + 11 = 14	11 + 3 = 14
4 + 10 = 14	12 + 2 = 14
5 + 9 = 14	13 + 1 = 14
6 + 8 = 14	14 + 0 = 14
7 + 7 = 14	

On pages 8 and 9 let the students draw the missing sets of shapes, then complete the number sentences.

Turn to page 10. In activity 1, the sets have already been partitioned. Ask the students to complete the number sentences. Check that they are able to do so. For activities 2 and 3, the students should draw crosses or simple shapes in the sets and put in a partition line. They then write the missing numbers in the number sentences.

Unit 7 Subtraction

Pupil Book page 11

Materials
- 20 bottle-caps per students

Objectives

Students should be able to:

 subtract a one-digit number from numbers up to 20.

Suggested approach

Distribute 20 bottle-caps per students. Let the students count their bottle-caps, arranging them in various ways on their desk.

Write the following number sentence on the board: 18 – 7 =…. Ask the students to use their bottle-caps to work out the answer. Repeat to activity with different number sentences.

CD-Rom activity
- Subtraction

Draw 15 circles on the board. Ask a student to count the number of circles. Cross out 6 of the circles. Ask another student to count how many circles are left. Ask another student to write the corresponding number sentence on the board. They should write 15 – 6 = 9. Repeat the activity a number of times.

Ask the students to complete page 11 in Pupil Book B.

Units 8 and 9 Working with shapes

Pupil Book pages 12 and 13

Materials
- cut-outs of circles, squares, triangles and rectangles of different sizes and shapes
- scissors
- tracing paper
- spent matches

Objectives

Students should be able to:

- name and recognise basic 2D shapes
- count items up to nine
- recognise shapes in the environment
- distinguish between squares and rectangles.

Suggested approach

Turn to page 12. Use this page to revise the names of rectangles, circles and triangles. You can also use it to make sure that the students can distinguish colours. The activity requires the students to count the numbers of shapes of different colours found in the picture. Start with the yellow rectangle; work with the class to count all the yellow rectangles in the drawing. Once you are in agreement about the amount, write the numeral in the space provided. Let the students work in pairs to complete the rest of the activity.

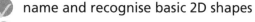

Display a square and invite individual students to name it. When the correct response is received, write the word 'square' on the board and draw the shape next to it. Repeat this procedure for the circle, the rectangle and the triangle. Show the students examples of differently shaped triangles, rectangles and other shapes. Turn to page 13. Give the students some time to look around the classroom and find examples of the shapes shown. As they find an example allow them to draw a tick on the shape. Once they have done this, let them draw their own shape, picture or pattern at the bottom of the page. Use this to assess how well they understand the basic characteristics of shapes. Do not focus too much on accurate drawing of shapes; rather check that their squares have more or less four equal sides, their triangles have three sides, their circles are round, and so on.

Unit 10   Lighter or heavier?

Pupil Book page 14

Materials
- a selection of light and heavy objects
- flashcards with 'lighter' and 'heavier'
- a balance scale

Objectives
Students should be able to:

 use the terms 'lighter' and 'heavier' with confidence

 estimate which objects are 'lighter' or 'heavier' in a set.

Suggested approach

The students should work practically and gain experience of working with mass before moving on to the written work.

Ask the students to choose pairs of objects from those that you have brought. Let them compare the mass of the objects by holding one in each hand. They should already know the terms 'heavier' and 'lighter', but if they do not, display the words on flashcards. If you have a balance scale, demonstrate to the class how it works. Make sure they understand that the pan that is down holds the heavier object. Allow students to estimate which is heavier or lighter in a pair of objects and then have them measure using the balance scale to check.

Turn to page 14. Focus on the picture of the girl in the middle of the page. Ask the class to name some things that are lighter than a girl. Then ask them to name some things that are heavier than a girl. Focus then on the objects around the girl. Explain to the class that they are to circle the objects that are lighter than the girl and colour the objects that are heavier.

Units 11 and 12   Time

Pupil Book pages 15 and 16

Objectives

Students should be able to:

 develop the skill of telling the time on the hour using both analogue and digital clocks

 relate time to their own activities.

Suggested approach

Have the students count from one to twelve and display the number symbol cards to correspond with the numbers. If the students do not know eleven and twelve, write these symbols on the board and have the students practise writing them.

Draw a large circle on the board. Write in the numerals from 1 to 12 in the positions they appear on a clock. Draw some blank digital clock faces as well.

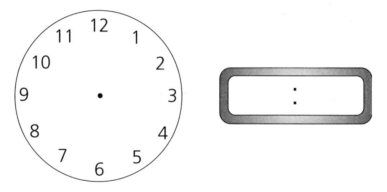

Discuss the two different kinds of clocks and where they are found.

Display your large clock. Point to some of the numerals and let the students say what they are. Show the class the hands of the clock. Ask: What do you notice about the hands? (One is longer than the other.)

If you have a real clock, let the class listen to it as it works and ask them what it is doing. (It is telling the time.) Ask the students questions about what time they get up, when they go to bed, when they go to school, and so on.

Show the class some of the times on your clock. If school begins at nine o'clock, show them 9 o'clock. Also write 9:00 on the digital clock. Explain that time looks different on the standard clock and the digital clock.

Let the students make 9 o'clock on their matchbox clocks. Check to see that they have managed it.

Write 'o'clock' on the board and ask a student to write 9 before it. Let another student record the same time on the digital clock.

Repeat this for several times on the hour that are meaningful to the students.

Go round and help the students make the time on their matchbox clocks. Soon they will realise that the long hand is always on the 12 when time is on the hour.

Put away your large clock and then have the class show a time on their own clocks. Get them to write down the times they make.

Turn to page 15. Have the students take turns to read the times shown on the clocks in section 1. Let them read and then write the times in section 2.

Turn to page 16. Let the students say what is happening in each scene. Discuss at what time these events are likely to take place. Let the students agree on a time for each event and then have them draw hands on the clocks to show the time. Check that they draw a long and short hand and that they represent the time fairly accurately. Stick to time on the hour at this stage.

Additional activities

Repeat some of the introductory activities above to give students more practise in telling the time. For example:

- Write a time in words on the board, such as 'eleven o'clock', and have the students draw this time into blank clock faces.
- Have the students come up to move the clock hands to show a given time.
- Write three different times on the board, and have the students select the correct one for a particular event. For example:
- waking up on school days (9 o'clock, 7 o'clock or 11 o'clock in the morning)
  - school roll call (8.30, 11.30 or 10.30 in the morning)
  - dinner time (4 o'clock, 7 o'clock or 11 o'clock).

Unit 13 Combining sets of money

Pupil Book page 17

Materials

- groups of objects for demonstration
- real coins/play money

Objectives

Students should be able to:

 combine sets to make amounts to nine.

Suggested approach

Note: This page will need to be adapted to meet the needs of your territory. For example, in Jamaica this lesson serves only to ensure that children understand that one-cent pieces are combined to make ten cents, although these small denomination coins are not used.

Revise combining objects to make sets.

Turn to page 17. If necessary and possible, give the students real coins or play money to model the situations. Let them fill in the numerals and then read the sentences aloud as a class. Check their number sentences to ensure that they are correct.

Unit 14 Counting coins

Pupil Book page 18

Materials
- one-cent, two-cent, five-cent and ten-cent coins for each student (real or play coins)
- flashcards showing various amounts

Objectives

Students should be able to:

 name and combine coins up to ten cents.

Suggested approach

Revise counting coins with students using flashcards. Show them a card with an amount on it and have them put together the required amount. Encourage them to try different combinations to get to the amount.

Once you have revised the concept, let the students complete page 18 independently, modelling answers using coins if they need to. Check the completed work to ensure that all students are able to do this.

Units 15 to 18 Ordinal numbers

Pupil Book pages 19 to 22

Materials
- tin cans
- ten index cards labelled 'first' to 'tenth'
- safety pins

Objectives

Students should be able to:

 use ordinal numbers from first to tenth

 give the position of objects in an array.

Suggested approach

Ask three students to come to the front of the class. Let the student who arrives first stand in front, the second student behind the first, and then the third student behind the second. Ask: Who is standing in front? (The class should call out the first student's name, for example, John.) Why is John standing in front? (Because he was the first to come up.) Pin the index card labelled 'first' onto the first student. Ask: Why is Ruth next in line? (Because she was second to come up. Peter was the third to come up.)

Repeat the activity with four students, and again with five students, using the words first, second, third, fourth and fifth, and pinning the relevant card on each student.

Put the cans on your desk. Point to the first can and say: This is the first can. Let individual students come up to the front and show the second can, third can, and so on.

Then draw ten bananas on the board (in a row). Let students point to the first, second, third, and so on. Say: This is the first banana. This is the second banana (up to the tenth banana). Each time, let a student put the correct card below each banana. Read through the words on the index cards as a class in order from first to tenth.

Take the students outside and place them in groups of ten. Let them run a short race (integrate with physical education) and give themselves positions.

Turn to page 19. Ask individual students to describe what they see in the picture. Say the position of each child as a class. Ask the class to say what colour T-shirt the first child is wearing. (Red.) Have them select a red crayon and colour the T-shirt that shows first. Let them complete the rest of the activity on their own.

Turn to page 20. Look at the first group of children. Point to the one on the right, say: This girl is first. Say the positions of the other children as you point to them. Let the students point to the girl who is second. Have them circle the second girl. Repeat this for the other three groups of children.

Read the ordinal positions (first, second, third, and so on) and ask the students to name the colours as you say the position. Next, read the letters from A to H. Instruct the students to colour the letters to match the positions.

Ask the students to identify the first letters of their names and surnames. Let them write these down. Explain that they can use these to make a pattern. Let them make their own patterns and complete them.

Turn to page 21. Point out that one object has been circled in each set. Make sure that the students are aware that each set starts at the right because the objects are facing that way. Do the activity orally first and then have the students write the positions. This further revises numeral formation.

CD-Rom activity
■ Ordinal numbers

Turn to page 22. Use the snake activity to assess the students' ability to read ordinal numbers. If you like, you can assess how well students listen to instructions by doing the activity as a listening task.

Unit 19 Looking back

Pupil Book page 23

Objectives

Students should be able to:

- subtract a one-digit number from numbers up to 20
- use several devices and strategies to build up the basic number facts for addition and subtraction
- count in sequence to 50
- compare the mass of two objects using phrases such as 'heavier than', 'lighter than' etc
- tell the time on the hour.

Suggested approach

This is a review lesson, which covers the skills and knowledge taught in the preceding units.

Read the instructions to the class. Let the students attempt the questions. Give guidance only as necessary. When the students have completed the Pupil Book page, discuss each of the questions and answers with them.

Note which students have difficulty and reinforce or reteach concepts as necessary.

Unit 20 How much have you learned?

Pupil Book page 24

Objectives

Students should be able to:

- tell the time on the hour
- compare the mass of two objects using phrases such as 'heavier than', 'lighter than' etc
- use the symbols <, > and = correctly
- identify ordinal positions
- use several devices and strategies to build up the basic number facts for addition and subtraction.

Suggested approach

This is an assessment lesson in which the students are tested on the concepts taught in the previous units.

Read the instructions to the class, so they all know what they have to do. When the students have completed the Pupil Book page, discuss each of the questions and answers with them.

Note which students have difficulty. You may want to give these students extra practice with these concepts.

Unit 21　More counting

Pupil Book page 25

Materials
- 50 sticks per group

> **Objectives**
>
> Students should be able to:
>
> count in sequence to 50.

Suggested approach

Review the method of tallying tens and ones by counting out collections of sticks (bundles of tens and ones) and asking the students to write up tallies on the board. They should also write the number and say the number name for each example you work through. Then read through the instructions for page 25 and ask the students to complete it.

Units 22 to 25　Counting in 2s and 5s

Pupil Book pages 26 to 29

Materials
- a half hundred square for each group or pair of students
- 50 bottle-caps

> **Objectives**
>
> Students should be able to:
>
> count in 2s and 5s to 50.

Suggested approach

Draw a number line on the board from 0 to 20. Use it to introduce counting in 2s. Ask the students what they will land on if they start at 0 and jump two spaces. (2.) Ask them to keep going, jumping in 2s, from 2 to 4 to 6 and so on.

Ask a student what they will land on if they start on 6 and move forward by 2 spaces. (8.) Ask a student what they will land on if the jump back 2 spaces from 18. (16.)

Ask the students to colour in every second number on their half hundred squares. Ask half the groups to start at 1 and the other half to start at 2.

Ask the students to group their bottle-caps into groups of two. Tell them that they are going to count in two using their bottle-caps. Help them at first to count: 2, 4, 6, 8, and so on.

Draw a set of simple bicycles on the board (for example five). Ask the students how many wheels there are on one bicycle. (Two.) Tell the students that they are now going to count in twos to find how many wheels there are altogether. Repeat a number of times, using different objects and pictures. If the students have difficulty at first counting twos, let them use their half hundred square. Eventually though they should be able to count in 2s without using the square.

Ask the students to complete pages 26 and 27 of Pupil Book B.

Repeat the above activities, this time counting in fives. As an introduction, you could get the class to count in fives orally. Tell the class that they are going to count in fives, and instead of using bottle-caps to help them, they are going to use fingers. Get a volunteer to hold up one hand and ask the class: How many fingers? (Five.) How many fives? (One.) Tell the volunteer to hold up the other hand. Ask: Now how many fives can you see? (Two.) Count in fives with the class: five, ten. Then ask another volunteer to add another hand. Say: Now there are three fives. Count with the class: five, ten, fifteen. Keep adding more students to the group holding up a hand at a time, and count in fives together with the class.

Give individual students the chance to try to count in fives as far as they can. Once you are sure that the students have mastered counting in fives, read through page 28 with them and let them work individually.

Before asking students to do page 29, explain the tally marks at the top of the page to them. Explain that arranging the marks like this (four upright and one line through the set of four) makes counting large numbers much easier. Demonstrate this on the board by drawing 20 vertical lines and underneath drawing four sets of tally marks. Tell the students that both these lines contain 20 marks. Ask them which line they think is easier to read.

Students can then complete page 29.

Units 26 and 27 Sets to 20

Pupil Book pages 30 and 31

Materials
- 20 two-colour discs in a paper bag for each group

Objectives
Students should be able to:
 represent numbers and perform additions to 20.

Suggested approach

Arrange the class in groups of a convenient size and distribute ten discs, a paper bag and a sheet of plain paper to each group. Let the students take turns in shaking the bag and throwing the discs onto the desk; let other students in the group count, describe and record on a piece of paper the number of discs with each colour side up. For example:

Six blue and four red make ten discs.

6 + 4 = 10   4 + 6 = 10

Let the students continue this activity until they have as many combinations of ten as they can find. If you like, add more discs to the bag and repeat this activity finding combinations of 20.

Draw 15 objects on the board. Ask one of the students to draw a circle around ten objects. Ask another student to say how many are left outside the circle. (Five.) Show how this can be written as 15, using a tens and ones table.

Let the students set out 17 discs and put ten of them together. Ask how many are left. (Seven.) The students should then record this as 17. Repeat with all the other numbers from eleven to 19. Encourage the students to read out these numbers to ensure that they know the names.

Complete the activities on page 30 by getting the students to draw the missing sets and then complete the number sentences. Allow them to use counters to model sets if they need to.

Turn to page 31. Explain to the class that they are going to draw crosses to represent groups of counters. Demonstrate the first two examples by setting out counters and then drawing crosses to represent them. When you are sure that the students know they are to place the correct number of objects in the sets to make a number sentence true, let them complete the activity on their own.

Unit 28 Three groups

Pupil Book page 32

Materials
- twelve bottle-caps per student

Objectives

Students should be able to:

 develop methods of adding three numbers.

Suggested approach

Write 2 + 3 + 4 on the board, and say: Let's use our bottle-caps to do what this number sentence says. Ask: What does it tell us to do? (This tells us to start with two.) Put two bottle-caps on your desk. Ask: What does it tell us next? (It tells us to add three.) Put three more bottle-caps on your desk. Ask: What does it tell us next? (Add four.) Let the students put four more bottle-caps on the desk. The arrangement should look something like this:

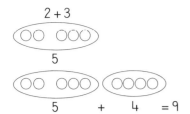

$2 + 3$

5

$5 + 4 = 9$

Show the students how to perform this addition in two steps. Draw the pattern of bottle-caps on the board and demonstrate how to add 2 + 3 to get 5. Show this as on the left. Point to the number sentence again and explain that you still have to add four. Again show this using the diagram and a number sentence as on the left.

Turn to page 32. Encourage the students to model each addition using bottle-caps and then have them write the number sentences. Check to see that they are able to do this.

Unit 29   Basic operations

Pupil Book page 33

> **Objectives**
>
> Students should be able to:
>
> - recognise odd and even numbers
> - recognise and practise basic addition facts.

Suggested approach

Discuss the number line with the students. Ask: Why are some numbers above the number line? (These are odd numbers.) What is special about the numbers below the line? (Except for 0, these are even numbers.) Have the students complete the additions and colour the chart accordingly. Allow them to check each other's work and to correct any mistakes.

Unit 30   Number line subtraction

Pupil Book page 34

> **Objectives**
>
> Students should be able to:
>
> - subtract single-digit numbers from numbers between 11 and 20 using a number line.

Suggested approach

Draw a number line from 0 to 20 on the board. Use this to demonstrate the examples at the top of page 34 to the students. For example, for the first one, start at 14 and use a chalk line to count 6 places back to show the students that you land on 8. Write the number sentence underneath. Explain the second example in the same way.

Write the sentence $15 - 3 = 12$ on the board. Ask a student to demonstrate this on the number line. Repeat a number of times.

Write the number sentence 20 – 3 = … on the board. Ask a student to use the number line to find the answer. Repeat a number of times with different students and different number sentences.

Ask the students to complete page 34 of Pupil Book B.

Unit 31 Calculator sums

Pupil Book page 35

Materials
■ calculators

Objectives
Students should be able to:

 use a calculator to demonstrate relationships among number facts for addition and subtraction.

Suggested approach

Show the class a calculator. Ask questions about the calculator to make sure that they remember how to use it. You can do this by asking questions about the purpose of each key on the calculator. As the students answer the questions, get them to show, explain or demonstrate what they have said.

Show the students how to key in some simple addition and subtraction problems. Call out some simple addition and subtraction problems and get the class to call out the answers.

Give the students opportunities to write their own simple sums. They can exchange these, solve each other's sums, then exchange gain and check each other's answers.

Turn to page 35 of Pupil Book B and ask the students to complete the problems in this unit.

Unit 32 Shapes

Pupil Book page 36

Materials
■ geoboards and rubber bands

Objectives
Students should be able to:

 use trial and error to investigate 2D shapes.

Suggested approach

Arrange the class in groups of four to six students and distribute a geoboard and some rubber bands to each group. Instruct the class that they are to make a triangle with a rubber band. Then, using a different rubber band, they are to make another triangle the same as the first triangle, but with a different orientation. Ask them how many other ways they can find to make triangles. Repeat the activity with different shapes.

Pupil Book page 36 provides the opportunity to record some of the shapes that students have found using the geoboards. They may find this activity easier if they first enlarge the dots they wish to use as corners, and then draw lines to join these larger dots. Encourage the students to talk about the shapes the make, using any mathematical names they know (for example, triangle, square, rectangle).

Unit 33 Patterns

Pupil Book page 37

Materials
- various items for making patterns, for example, string, wool, pasta shapes, shells, seeds, scraps of material
- glue
- pieces of card

Objectives
Students should be able to:
 explore patterns using regular shapes and environmental objects
 appreciate the idea of symmetry.

Suggested approach

Discuss page 37 fully with the class. Have the students work through the activities in groups. You might find it useful to work together with the students rather than letting them work on their own at first.

Discuss the items in the 'talk about' box. Give each group pieces of string or wool, different pasta shapes, shells, seeds and scraps of material. Allow them to choose the objects that they like best and use them to make a pattern by gluing the items onto pieces of card. Display the completed patterns in the classroom.

Make observations about the students' patterns and pictures. (For example, some two-dimensional shapes make patterns that cover an entire page, whilst some patterns have more spaces in between the shapes.)

Unit 34 Picture graphs

Pupil Book page 38

Objectives
Students should be able to:
 read and interpret simple picture graphs.

Suggested approach

Turn to page 38. Explain to the students that they are going to be reading a graph that shows how many fruits are in a bowl. Explain that one picture represents one fruit. Let the students identify the names of the fruits and say what each picture stands for.

Let the students use the graph to answer oral questions about the graph, for example: How many limes are there? How many more limes are there than bananas? And so on.

Let the students complete activity 1 independently. When they have done this, have them look at activity 2 and discuss how you would add the fruit on the plate to the graph. Let them draw fruits to represent those shown. They can complete activity 3 on their own. Check that all students have the correct answers.

Unit 35 Bar graphs

Pupil Book page 39

Materials
■ collections of two types of objects, e.g. pens and pencils, or lollipop sticks and matches

Objectives
Students should be able to:
- describe how data is presented in a bar graph
- read and interpret data represented in bar graphs
- describe similarities and differences between pictographs and bar graphs.

Suggested approach

Ask about nine students (boys and girls) to stand in two columns in front of the class - boys in one row, girls in another. The students in the two columns should stand exactly next to each other. Ask questions such as:
■ How many boys are there?
■ How many girls are there?
■ How many students are there altogether?
■ Which row is longer?
■ Which row is shorter
■ Are there more or less girls than boys?
■ How many more/less girls are there than boys?

Encourage the students to focus on the longer line as the line with more students. Draw a representation on the board as shown.

Redraw this graph in the style as the graph on page 39. Make sure that you clearly label the axes and give the graph a title. Tell the students that this graph shows the same information as the picture you previously drew. Ask students questions about the graph to make sure that they understand what it shows.

Turn to page 39 and discuss the graph with the students. Make sure that they know what the graph shows by asking them questions about it. They can then complete the questions in this unit.

column graph

Unit 36 Length

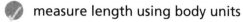

Pupil Book page 40

Materials
- small lengths of ribbon

Objectives

Students should be able to:

- measure length using body units
- understand why standard units are necessary.

Suggested approach

It is important that students get lots of practice with practical measuring before they move on to pen and paper working. They have already compared objects by length using estimation and visual discrimination. In this unit they will start to compare objects in terms of informal units of measure, finger widths and feet lengths.

Demonstrate to the class how to measure using finger widths. Select several small objects in the classroom. First ask the students to estimate how many finger widths they think these objects measure. Then let the students practise measuring them in fingers.

Give each group several lengths of ribbon (number them or identify them in some way). Ask the students to measure the pieces of ribbon using their fingers and to record how long each piece is. Collect the pieces of ribbon and redistribute them randomly. Ask the students to look at them and guess (estimate) how many finger widths long they think each piece will be. Explain that this is called estimating and that estimating is an important part of learning to measure. By estimating we can get an idea of what the answer should be.

Ask the students to measure the pieces of ribbon that they have and compare their answers to the students who first measured the pieces of ribbon. Ask the students if they notice anything. The students may notice that some of the measurements are different. Explain to them that this is why we have standard units of measurement. Explain that they will learn about these later. The standard units make sure that everyone knows what you mean when you say that something is 1 m long. If they say it is 1 hand width long, you would not know exactly how long it was because their hand width might be much wider than yours.

When you are satisfied that the students can measure in finger widths, turn to page 40 and have them complete section 1.

Repeat the practical measuring activity using feet. Let the students physically measure various objects in the classroom. Again, encourage them to estimate before they measure. When you are satisfied that they can do this have them complete section 2.

Unit 37   How heavy?

Pupil Book page 41

Materials
- interlocking cubes or marbles
- pens, small balls, small scissors, sweets, rulers, tubes of glue, crayons, keys, apples
- balance scales

Objectives

Students should be able to:

 estimate and measure the mass of objects using non-standard units.

Suggested approach

Choose two different objects that are obviously different in mass. Ask the class which they think is heavier. Let them hold the objects if necessary. Ask a student to put the objects on the scales to check.

Repeat this process for different pairs of objects.

Put one of the objects on one side of the balance scales. Ask the students how many cubes they think they will need to balance the scales. Let them all have a guess. Ask a student to check how many cubes are needed.

Repeat using different objects. The students should first guess the mass of each object in cubes before they use the balance scales to find the answer.

Ask students to complete page 41 of Pupil Book B.

Unit 38   How much money?

Pupil Book page 42

Materials
- five-cent, two-cent and one-cent coins for each group
- matchboxes

Objectives

Students should be able to:

 use combinations of coins to make totals up to 25c.

Suggested approach

Note: One-cent and five-cent coins are not used in Jamaica. However it is important that you make play coins, as the students still need to visualise that 100 cents are equal to one dollar.

Give each group of students their coins in a matchbox. Ask them to show you the five-cent coin. Check that they have chosen the correct one. Repeat using the two-cent coin and the one-cent coin.

Instruct the students to take out different combinations of coins from the matchboxes. Start with an easy combination such as: Take out three one-cent coins. Ask: How much does that make? (Three cents.) Check that the students are able to identify the amount as three cents. Repeat using different combinations of coins. You may like to extend the activity to use these three coins in various combinations, up to a total of 25c.

Have the students turn to page 42. Look at the pictures of coins. Discuss the questions in the 'talk about' box. The coins shown come from Jamaica, the OECS, Trinidad and Tobago, and Barbados. We can tell where a coin comes from because it has the name of the territory printed on it.

Let the students complete the addition work. In each example the students are to write the numeral for the total amount of money shown on the left.

Unit 39 Looking back

Pupil Book page 43

Objectives

Students should be able to:

- interpret data represented in simple pictographs
- compare the capacity of containers
- use objects to determine the missing number in an addition number sentence
- complete number patterns.

Suggested approach

This is a review lesson, which covers the skills and knowledge taught in the preceding units.

Read the instructions to the class. Let the students attempt the questions. Give guidance only as necessary. When the students have completed the Pupil Book page, discuss each of the questions and answers with them.

Note which students have difficulty and reinforce or reteach concepts as necessary.

Unit 40 How much have you learned?

Pupil Book page 44

> ### Objectives
> Students should be able to:
> - interpret data represented in simple bar graphs
> - compare the mass of objects using non-standard units
> - count in twos
> - use a number line to subtract two numbers.

Suggested approach

This is an assessment lesson in which the students are tested on the concepts taught in the previous units.

Read the instructions to the class, so they all know what they have to do. When the students have completed the Pupil Book page, discuss each of the questions and answers with them.

Note which students have difficulty. You may want to give these students extra practice with these concepts.

Unit 41 Number names

Pupil Book page 45

Materials
- domino cards with numerals and number names

> ### Objectives
> Students should be able to:
> - recognise and read number names to twenty
> - match number names to given sets.

Suggested approach

Place the students in small groups and allow them to play games with the domino cards. They can play matching games where the cards are dealt out randomly and they take turns to put a card on the table. The student who has the matching card, that is, the numeral or the number name, plays it and then has another turn.

They can also play ordering games, using just the number name cards. Deal the cards out randomly, and choose one student to start. That student plays any card. The next in line must place the number following or preceding it. If they cannot, they skip a turn. The winner is the person to get rid of their cards first.

The students should be able to complete page 45 with little or no hesitation. Observe them carefully as they work and assist those who have difficulty

Units 42 and 43 Counting to 100

Pupil Book pages 46 and 47

Objectives

Students should be able to:

 count in sequence to 100.

Suggested approach

Draw a set of ten crosses on the board. Ask the students to count the crosses. Ask: How many tens? (One.) How many ones? (None.) Get the students to write this in a tally chart, and to write the numeral underneath. Do the same with twenty, thirty, forty, and so on, up to 100, introducing the class to the vocabulary. Students have already covered counting to 50, so only 60 to 100 will be new to them.

Divide the class into groups and give each group a bag containing 100 sticks and ten lengths of thread. Let each group begin to make bundles of ten sticks. After a few minutes, stop the activity and ask one of the groups how many bundles of ten it has made. For example, the group may have wrapped three bundles. Ask how many sticks that is (30.) Emphasise that three tens are thirty and so on.

In their groups, ask the students to make a chart containing all the numerals from 1 to 100. Give each group a sheet of card divided into 100 squares (10 × 10). The students should fill in the numerals 1 to 100 in the correct order.

Ask the students to turn to page 46. Ask a volunteer to read out the first ten numbers on the hundred square. Get another volunteer to read out the next ten numbers. Emphasise that we read from left to right starting with the top row. Ask the students questions about the grid, for example:
- What is one less than 25? … 49? … 77? etc.
- What is one more than 43? … 67? … 89? etc.
- What number is between 48 and 50? … 95 and 97? etc.

Once you feel that the students are comfortable with numbers up to 100, ask them complete pages 46 and 47.

Unit 44   Calculator counting

Pupil Book page 48

Materials
- calculators

Objectives

Students should be able to:

 use calculators to count in a variety of ways.

Suggested approach

Turn to page 48 of Pupil Book B. Work through the example in the blue box with the students. Ask the students to press these keys 0 + 2 =, and ask them what answer the calculator shows. Ask them to press = again, and tell you what the calculator shows this time.

Ask the students how many times that would have to press the = key to get to 10 if they started with 0 + 2.

Ask the students how they would count in 2s starting from 12. (They should type in 12 + 2 +.)

As a class, discuss how they could use their calculators to count in 5s and 10s. The students should realise that they should follow the same principle, but to count in 5s they should type in 0 + 5 =, and to count in 10s they should type in 0 + 10 =.

Ask students to complete the activities on page 48 of Pupil Book B.

Draw the students' attention to the 'talk about' box on page 48. Help them to realise that to count backwards means taking away numbers. They should be able to tell you that they can use the same method to count backwards that they used to count forwards, except this time they have to use the – key.

Unit 45 to 48   Repeated counting

Pupil Book pages 49 to 52

Materials
- 20 bottle-caps per student

Objectives

Students should be able to:

 use objects and pictures/diagrams to show repeated addition situations

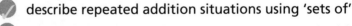 describe repeated addition situations using 'sets of'

write number sentences to represent repeated addition situations.

Suggested approach

Put a pile of bottle-caps on your desk. Ask one of the students to come forward and give you two of the bottle-caps, then two more, then two more, and then two more. Ask: How many times did you give me two bottle-caps? How many have you given me altogether?

Ask another student to write the number sentence that describes what the previous student did. (2 + 2 + 2 + 2 = 8.) Repeat the procedure using 3, 4, 5 and 10.

Write this number sentence on the board: 5 groups of 2 make …. Ask a student to carry out the following steps:
■ Draw a picture to represent the number sentence.
■ Complete the number sentence. (2 + 2 +2 + 2 + 2 = 10.)
■ Read the number sentence aloud.

Ask the class to use their bottle tops to make three sets of two, and to work out the total. Repeat this procedure several times.

Instruct students to complete the activities on page 49 of Pupil Book B.

Draw a number line from 0 to 20 on the board. Tell the students that they can also use a number line to do repeated addition. Draw three jumps on your number line like this:

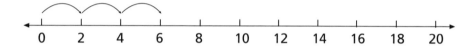

0	2	4	6	8	10	12	14	16	18	20

Ask a students to explain what this shows. (Three jumps of two.) Ask another student to write this as a number sentence on the board.

Repeat with similar examples, adding 3, 4, 5 and 10 a number of times.

Ask students to do page 50 of Pupil Book B.

Ask the students to make two sets of three bottle-caps and find the answer. Ask them to write down this number sentence. Then ask them to make three sets of three bottle-caps and again write down the answer and number sentence. Repeat this exercise a few more times. Ask them if they notice a pattern in their answers. (They increase by 3 each time.) This should be clearer after the students have completed page 52.

Instruct the students to complete the activities on pages 51 and 52 of Pupil Book B.

Unit 49 Collecting data

Pupil Book page 53

Objectives

Students should be able to:

 collect simple sets of data through simple interviews

record collected data using simple number statements.

Students have already come across the tally marks used on page 53. If you think it is necessary, revise the concept of making tally marks in groups of 5 to make it easier to count large numbers.

Turn to page 53. Read through the instructions for activities 1 and 2. Make sure the students understand what they have to do. For activity 1, students have to ask their friends which fruits they like best. You may want to give the students of maximum number of people they can ask.

In activity 2, students have to talk to their friends to find the information that they need to complete the table. Do not worry if the class gets quite noisy for a while, as students will be talking to each other to find out the data they need for their tables.

Instruct the students to complete the activities on page 53 of Pupil Book B.

Unit 50 Hot, cold or warm

Pupil Book page 54

Materials
- ice
- kettle
- water
- cups

Objectives

Students should be able to:

 describe the temperature of an object using phrases such as 'warm', 'hot', 'cold', etc.

Suggested approach

Have a discussion with the students about hot and cold. Talk about the weather, about the hottest and coldest things that the students can think of. Encourage the students to talk comparatively about hot and cold. For example, a cup of tea is hot, but the sun is far hotter, rain is cool, but ice is cold, and so on.

Using the kettle, make cups of water that are very different temperatures, for example boiling water, warm water cool water and ice cold water. You can ask students feel the outside of the cups and describe the temperatures relative to each other.

Students can then complete page 54 of Pupil Book B.

Unit 51 Litres

Pupil Book page 55

Materials
- different sizes of containers
- sand and/or water
- a plastic one litre bottle and a 250 ml plastic cup for each group

Objectives

Students should be able to:
- understand and use the terms 'full' and 'empty'
- use standard units to measure capacity
- understand and use the term 'litres'.

Before you tackle the material in the Pupil Book you need to have a practical lesson using as many different types and sizes of containers as possible. Working outside, give the students various tasks to get them familiar with the concepts of full, empty, half-full. .

Students have already done some practical activities involving capacity, but they have not worked with standard units, even at an informal level. Introduce this concept by demonstrating that it is possible to use a cup to fill up a bottle. Pour one cup of liquid into a litre bottle. Then point out that the bottle is now quarter-full. Ask the class what they think will happen if you pour the other cup in. Ask: Do you think one more cup will fill the bottle? (Note which students say yes.) Pour in another cup of liquid and ask: Is the bottle full yet? (No. It is only half-full.) Repeat the procedure until the bottle is full. Represent what you have done on the board by drawing number sentences using cups and bottles as on Pupil Book page 55.

Hand out objects similar to the ones on page 55 and ask the students whether they would measure these in cups or bottles. Check that they give sensible answers. Give each group a 250 ml cup and a litre bottle. Let them fill the containers with water and then draw cups or bottles to show how much each container holds.

Additional activities

Students may sometimes refer to a container as half-full, or half-empty. Tell the students to stop you when the cup is half-full. Pour water slowly into a cup, until the cup is half-full. Then fill another cup with water, and have a student come up and pour out water until it is half-empty. Ask:

- Which cup is half-full?
- Which cup is half-empty?

Then mix the cups up, and ask:

- Now which cup is half-full, and which is half-empty?

The students should realise that half-full and half-empty are, in fact, the same, although they may tend to use half-full when *filling* a container, and half-empty when *emptying* it.

Unit 52   What units do we use?

Pupil Book page 56

Materials
- several flash cards with 'metres' and 'litres'
- magazine pictures to illustrate capacity and length

Objectives

Students should be able to:

 select the appropriate unit for measuring.

Suggested approach

Place the magazine pictures on the board. Hand out flash cards to several students. Ask them to read the word on their flash cards. Instruct one student to come up to the board and choose an object that would be measured in the unit shown on their flash card. Let them stick the cards below the object they have chosen and ask the others to confirm that this is the correct unit.

Remove all the pictures and flash cards. Arrange the pictures on your desk face down. Stick the flash cards onto the board. Let the students take turns to come up, turn over a picture, decide what unit it will be measured in and stick the picture above a flash card with that unit on it.

Turn to page 56. Discuss what is shown in each photograph. Let the students select the correct unit and circle it. Walk around and check that they are able to do this.

Units 53 and 54 Mass

Pupil Book pages 57 and 58

Materials
- various objects for weighing (see activities) including a big paper bag full of leaves or crumpled paper and a smaller but heavier bag of sand
- objects that could be considered heavy
- a balance scale
- an object weighing exactly 1 kg or a 1 kg mass piece

Objectives
Students should be able to:

 use a balance scale to measure and compare mass

 recognise and use the kilogram as a standard unit of mass.

Suggested approach

Show the class the 1 kg object that you have brought. Explain to them that we use kilograms to measure how heavy an object is. Write the word 'kilogram' and the abbreviation 'kg' on the board and practise reading them.

Explain to the class that you are going to compare objects to see whether they are heavier or lighter than 1 kg. Encourage them to suggest how you might do this.

Place the kilogram measure on one pan. Choose any other lighter object and place it on the other pan. Ask the class to say what has happened. (The kilogram has gone down and the other object has gone up, so it must be lighter.) Repeat this several times using both heavier and lighter objects. Have different students describe what is happening each time.

Turn to page 57. If you have enough balances, give each group one to work with. If not, place the balance and the 1 kg mass piece at the front and demonstrate the lesson. Let the students draw the objects in the correct columns as they are measured.

Turn to page 58. Explain to the class that the objects shown either weigh 1 kg or ½ kg. Let them discuss the objects and guess which objects weigh 1 kg. Have them write '1 kg' on the objects they choose. Let them write '½ kg' on the other objects.

Remind the class how to draw a block graph. Let them complete activity 2 on their own. Walk around and assist any students who are having problems. Praise those who are working well.

Units 55 and 56   Sorting solid shapes

Pupil Book pages 59 and 60

Materials
■ a variety of cube, cuboid, sphere shaped objects, boxes and balls (there must be a large and small object of each shape)

Objectives
Students should be able to:

 classify three-dimensional objects on the basis of their attributes, such as shape and/or size

 explain why a three-dimensional object can slide, roll or stack.

Suggested approach

Display the objects that you have brought to class one by one. Ask the class how they could place the shapes into groups. The students may just name two groups; those that are round and those that have straight sides. At this point this is enough.

Ask the students to explain why they have grouped the objects the way that they have.

Show the students the large sphere and the small sphere. Ask the students what is the same and what is different about the two objects you are holding up. They should be able to tell you that the two objects are the same shape, but they are different sizes. One is big and one is small. Repeat for the other pairs of objects.

Ask students to complete page 59 of Pupil Book B.

Ask the students of they know what sliding, rolling and stacking mean. Ask them to demonstrate with the appropriate shape.

Ask the students if they can stack spheres. Ask them to explain why they can or cannot. Students can try to stack the spheres, roll them and slide them.

Repeat for the other shapes. Students may get confused about the difference between rolling and sliding, especially when it comes to the

CD-Rom activity
- 3D shapes

spheres and cylinders. You may need to explain to them that rolling is when the shape moves by turning, and sliding is when the shape can move across the surface without turning. You may need to demonstrate this using a sphere and a cube.

Ask students to complete page 60.

Unit 57 Paying for things

Pupil Book page 61

Materials
- cardboard one-cent, two-cent, five-cent and ten-cent coins for the students to use

Objectives

Students should be able to:

 represent a coin value (up to 20c) using several combinations of coins.

Suggested approach

Arrange the students into small groups. Give each group a set of coins. Let the students name the value of the coins that they have. On the board, draw a picture of a packet of sweets and tell the students that it costs 15c. Ask the students how they could pay for the packet of sweets using the coins that they have. Once all the groups have finished, ask them how they used their coins to pay for the sweets. Write on the board the different combinations of coins that the groups used. This will help the students to see that there are different combinations of coins they can use to make the same amount.

If the groups all used the same combination of coins, you will have to ask them to think of other ways to make up the same amount.

Repeat the activity using different totals. Then ask the students to complete page 61 of Pupil Book B.

Unit 58 How much does it cost?

Pupil Book page 62

Materials
- classroom shop
- 1c, 5c and 10c play coins

Objectives

Students should be able to:

 combine and partition using coin amounts

 understand the concept of giving change.

Suggested approach

Turn to page 62. Discuss the picture with the class. Talk about how much each item might cost realistically in your territory. Agree on prices as a class and let the students write these down next to each item. Decide as a class how much money you will give each child and draw the amounts. Use the prices that you decided earlier to decide what each child could buy.

Unit 59 Looking back

Pupil Book page 63

> ### Objectives
> Students should be able to:
> use number lines to count in 2s, 3s, 5s and 10s.

Suggested approach

This is a review lesson, which covers the skills and knowledge taught in the preceding units.

Read the instructions to the class. Let the students attempt the questions. Give guidance only as necessary. When the students have completed the Pupil Book page, discuss each of the questions and answers with them.

Note which students have difficulty and reinforce or reteach concepts as necessary.

CD-Rom activity
- Skip counting

Note: Allow students to use a number line for this activity.

Unit 60 How much have you learned?

Pupil Book page 64

> ### Objectives
> Students should be able to:
>  identify which three-dimensional shapes can slide, roll or stack
>  estimate the mass of objects using the kilogram as the unit of measure
> represent a coin value using several combinations of coins.

Suggested approach

This is an assessment lesson in which the students are tested on the concepts taught in the previous units.

Read the instructions to the class, so they all know what they have to do. When the students have completed the Pupil Book page, discuss each of the questions and answers with them.

Note which students have difficulty. You may want to give these students extra practice with these concepts.

Units 61 and 62   Counting in 10s

Pupil Book pages 65 and 66

Materials
- paper bags containing a few less than 100 sticks and ten lengths of thread
- hundred charts
- crayons

Objectives
Students should be able to:

 count in 10s to 100.

Suggested approach

Divide the class into groups of three or four students and give each group a paper bag containing a few less than 100 sticks. Let the groups find out how many stick they have. To do this, each student in the group should wrap a set of ten sticks with thread, until there are not enough sticks left over to make a full set of ten. At this point, ask a member of a group to pick up the sets of ten, one by one, and count them aloud (10, 20, 30, and so on) and finally, to count the remaining sticks and tell you the total. Ask students from other groups to do the same.

Then ask the groups to find out how many more sticks they need to make 100. Give each group the number of sticks they need to make 100. Then let them wrap the single sticks they have to make the final set of ten. Ask one of the students in each group to pick up and count out the bundles of ten (10, 20, 30, up to 100).

Display a hundred chart and point to the numeral 40. Ask a member of each group to hold up that number of sticks (four bundles of ten). Then ask one of them to say that number. Next tell them to pick up ten more sticks and say how many they have now. Repeat with other multiples of ten.

Now let each of the groups use its own hundred chart. One member of each group should hold up one or more of the bundles of ten sticks. Another students should say how many sticks are in the first student's hand and pint to the corresponding number on the hundred chart. Ask a third student to point and say the number that is ten more than the number that has just been named.

Instruct students to do the activities on pages 65 and 66 of Pupil Book B.

Units 63 to 66   Multiplying by 2, 3 and 4

Pupil Book pages 67 to 70

Materials
■ 16 bottle-caps per student

Objectives
Students should be able to:

 complete multiplication number statements, with products up to 16

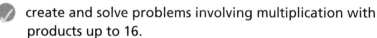 create and solve problems involving multiplication with products up to 16.

Suggested approach

Follow a similar teaching pattern as you used to teach units 45 to 48. Put a pile of bottle-caps on you desk. Then ask one of the students to come forward and to give you two of the bottle-caps, then two more, then two more, and then two more. Ask: How many times did you give me two bottle-caps? How many have you given me altogether?

Ask a student to write on the board the number sentence that describes what the previous student did ($4 \times 2 = 8$) and then to read it aloud. Repeat the procedure several times with different multiplication sums including multiplying by 2, 3 and 4. Include multiplication of 2, 3 and 4 by 0. Help the students to see that no matter what number you multiply by 0, the answer will always be 0.

Write this number sentence on the board: 5 groups of 2 make …. Ask a student to draw a picture to represent the number sentence, write the number sentence using the multiplication sign ($5 \times 2 = 10$) and to read the number sentence aloud.

Tell the students to make three sets of two, and to use their bottle-caps to work out the total. Repeat this procedure several times making sets of two, three and four.

Ask the students to complete the activities on pages 67 to 69 of Pupil Book B.

Tell the class to listen to the following number story: Every day, Mary collects three bottle-caps. How many did she collect altogether on Monday, Tuesday and Wednesday?

Next, break up the story into sections as follows. How many bottle caps did she collect each day? (Three.) On how many days did she collect bottle-caps? (Three.) How many did she collect altogether? (Nine.)

Make up several similar examples of your own.

Write the following pairs of incomplete number sentences on the board:

$2 \times 3 = …$ $3 \times 2 = …$
$4 \times 1 = …$ $1 \times 4 = …$
$2 \times 5 = …$ $5 \times 2 = …$

$4 \times 2 = \dots$ $2 \times 4 = \dots$
$1 \times 3 = \dots$ $3 \times 1 = \dots$

Let the students make two sets of bottle-caps to demonstrate 2×3 to find the answer. Ask a student to come forward and complete the number sentence on the board.

Then let the students to arrange their bottle-caps to show 3×2, and repeat the procedure. Ask: Is 2×3 the same as 3×2? Why? Students should realise that both number sentences give the same answers. Do the remaining exercises on the board in the same way.

Instruct students to complete page 70 of Pupil Book B.

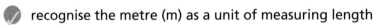

CD-Rom activity
- Multiplication

Units 67 and 68 Measuring in metres

Pupil Book pages 71 and 72

Materials
- a metre stick
- newspaper and scissors

Objectives

Students should be able to:

- recognise the metre (m) as a unit of measuring length
- estimate and measure lengths using standard units (m)
- record each of their estimates and measurements using the appropriate notation.

Suggested approach

Note: You probably need to practise making a metre stick from newspaper before the lesson in order to demonstrate it confidently to the class.

Introduce this lesson by talking about the picture on Pupil Book page 71. The 'talk about' box asks which child's arm we should use to measure. Discuss this with the class, explaining that we would get a different measurement from each child's arm. If you were buying, for example cloth, from a merchant and she was using her arm to measure it, you might choose the merchant with the longest arms! This raises the issue of standard measures and the need for standard units. Extend the discussion by asking the class what other body parts they could use to measure. For example, hand spans, finger lengths, finger widths, strides and footsteps.

Review measuring objects by allowing the students to use informal units to measure objects in the classroom. Remind the students of the need to leave no gaps when lining up the units of measure. Let the student estimate the length of the object they are measuring, and then measure by using the unit of measure repeatedly. Prepare a worksheet like the one below and have students complete it using paper clips as a standard but informal unit of measure.

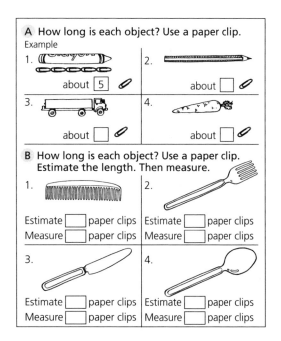

Explain to the students that we use standard units of measurement to avoid confusion and to make sure that everyone agrees about the length of different objects. Show the class what a metre stick looks like. Walk around with a metre stick, place it next to objects and ask questions such as: In this desk longer or shorter than a metre? Is Daniel shorter or taller than the metre stick?

Demonstrate to the class how to make their own metre length of newspaper. Follow the steps shown on page 71, including folding the strip in half, writing the student's name and a half ($1/2$) on the strip. Give the students plenty of opportunity to measure different objects in the classroom using their metre strips. Encourage them to estimate in metres before they measure and then to measure at least twice to check their estimates and get an accurate measurement. They should write down their estimates and measurements for each object that they measure.

You can take this activity further by asking the students to measure distances. For example they could estimate the length of the classroom or the playground in metres, and then use their own metre to measure these distances. They should also record each of their estimates and measurements using the appropriate notation.

Turn to page 72. Discuss with the class where you will find objects similar to the ones shown in the photographs. Also decide which child you will use for the height measurement. Once the students have finished the task, check the answers with them.

The graph on page 72 relates to the measurements above. Work through this as a class, asking questions to guide the students. For example, say: Look at your measurements. How many items are more than 1 m long? How many items are exactly 1 m long? How many items are less than 1 m long? Have the students colour blocks as you agree about the lengths.

Check the graphs to see that students have managed to complete them correctly.

Unit 69 Double and half

Pupil Book page 73

Materials
- paper and paints
- cut-out letters of the alphabet
- small mirrors

Objectives
Students should be able to:
- understand the concept of half
- begin to explore the concept of symmetry.

Suggested approach

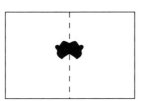

Give each student a sheet of paper. Walk around and place a blob of paint more or less in the middle of each paper. Demonstrate how to fold the paper to make a symmetrical shape.

Discuss the results. Make sure that the students realise that the design is the same on both sides of the fold. Let the students play with cardboard block letters and small mirrors to find out for themselves whether any of the letters are symmetrical. You will need to demonstrate how to place the mirror across the middle of the shapes. The students should work in pairs and discuss their findings as they work.

Turn to page 73. Let the students use the mirrors to find half of each shape and then colour it. They should be able to complete activity 2 on their own using the dotted lines to guide their drawing. Walk around as they are working and assist those who are struggling.

Units 70 and 71 One half and one quarter

Pupil Book pages 74 and 75

Materials
- rectangular and square pieces of paper
- crayons

Objectives
Students should be able to:
- identify one half and one quarter of a whole
- represent one half and one quarter of a whole
- read and write the fractions $\frac{1}{2}$ and $\frac{1}{4}$.

Suggested approach

Review with the students that one half means one part out of two equal parts. Distribute square sheets of paper. Let the students fold them in half in different ways and name each part.

Ask the students to fold the pieces of paper to show four equal parts. As students attempt this activity, move around the class, reminding them that for the parts to be equal, all the folded edges must touch. Assist those students who are having difficulties.

Ask the students to open their papers. The results should look like the ones on the next page.

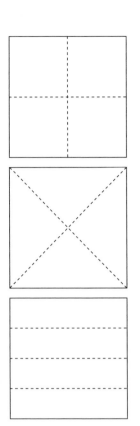

Ask the students how many equal parts they have, and what they would call each part. They should understand that they have four equal parts, each called 'one part out of four' or one quarter. Then give each student a rectangular piece of paper, and let them fold it to show quarters.

You can then ask the students to colour in one quarter of their shapes. Then ask them to colour in another section and ask them how much of the shape is now coloured in (two quarters).

Ask students to do page 74 of Pupil Book B.

Turn to Pupil Book page 75. Read through the information at the top of the page with the class. Then let the students work though some examples on the board as follows:

- Draw a circle on the board, and draw five radii dividing the circle into five equal parts.
- Ask a student to come up and shade one of the parts.
- Ask: How many parts are shaded. How many parts are there altogether?
- Ask the student to write the fraction.

Repeat the procedure with various fractions.

Once you are satisfied that the students are comfortable working with unit fractions, ask: How could we write the fraction if more than one part were shaded?

Get a student to come up a shade another two parts of the circle that had one fifth shaded. Ask: How many parts are there altogether? (Five.) How many are shaded? (Three.) How do we write this fraction? ($^3/_5$.) Repeat with a few more example, reminding the students that the top number in the fraction refers to the parts shaded and the bottom part is the total number of parts.

Ask students to do page 75 of Pupil Book B.

Units 72 and 73   Basic addition facts

Pupil Book pages 76 and 77

> ### Objectives
> Students should be able to:
> perform basic addition and subtraction
> recognise odd and even numbers.

Suggested approach

These units provide practice and consolidation of basic addition and subtraction facts. Read the instructions to the class and allow them to work independently through the activities. Check the answers and provide support and encouragement as necessary. Page 77 is a fun page.

Walk around as the students are working and help those who are struggling. Point out that the completed moth is the same on both sides.

Pupil Book pages 78 and 79

Materials
- a real clock
- large clock face

Objectives

Students should be able to:

 show how the hands of a clock move in relation to each other

 recognise and represent times on the hour and half-hour.

Suggested approach

Display the real clock with the hands showing one o'clock. Make sure that the students see the long hand pointing to twelve and the short hand to one. Keeping the clock face in full view, adjust the time to show two o'clock. Ask the class what they saw happening. (The minute hand went right round; the hour hand moved from twelve to two.) Establish that the time is two o'clock: one hour later than one o'clock.

Repeat the demonstration, moving the hands to about 2:15, then to about 2:30, then to about 2:45 and then to three o'clock. Each time you stop the hands, ask: Is the time two o'clock? Is it three o'clock? Only when the minute hand reaches twelve is the answer to the second question 'yes'. Record the o'clock times on the board.

Repeat this procedure until the clock shows five o'clock. Then ask: What comes one hour after five o'clock? (Six o'clock.) Invite one child to come and hold the real clock and another the model clock face. Ask the second student to arrange the hands of the model clock face so that they show a time one hour later than five o'clock. Check that he or she shows six o'clock.

Draw twelve digital clock faces on the board. Record two o'clock on the digital clock face as 2:00, explaining that this format of writing time is used on digital clocks. Ask the class: What comes one hour after two o'clock? Let a student record the time on the next digital clock face, using the notation demonstrated above. Repeat the activity, each time allowing a different student to record the time using digital notation.

Show the students that when the long hand is halfway round, the hour hand is halfway between one hour and the next. Let groups of students turn the hands of the real clock and watch both hands moving. Encourage them to talk about what they see. Let other students set the model clock at various half-hours, making sure that both hands are in the correct position. They could ask each other what times they have set.

Draw some digital faces on the board. Record half past two as 2:30. Explain that there are 60 minutes in one hour. This means that there are 30 minutes in half an hour. Ask a student to record the time for half an hour later on the next digital clock face. Repeat the activity, allowing a different student to record the time for the next half an hour using digital notation.

Turn to Pupil Book page 78. Let the students look at the left-hand clocks which show the time and say what the times are. Encourage them to relate those times to any meaningful events that take place in the day (breakfast, lunch, and so on). Let them write the times beneath each clock. Explain that they are going to fill in the time one hour later on the clocks on the right. Discuss what each time will be. Once you have reached agreement, the students draw hands and write the digital notation to show that time.

Turn to Pupil Book page 79. Complete activity 1 by having the students draw hands to show the time. Check that they are correct before moving on. In activity 2, students need to read time on the half-hour and write it down. Give help to the students that need it, particularly for activity 2.

Unit 76 Counting cents

Pupil Book page 80

Materials
- classroom shop
- 1c, 5c and 10c play coins

Objectives
Students should be able to:

 combine and partition using coin amounts

 understand the concept of giving change.

Suggested approach

Begin the lesson by playing 'shop', first selling single items and then sets of items provided that the cost is not more than 20c. If the class has had regular practice at shopping, this part of the lesson can be kept short.

Allow the students to keep only their 10c coins and to continue to come out and buy articles from you. Unless they buy objects costing 10c or 20c, they will need to be given change; otherwise they will be paying you too much. They will quickly realise this but it will take longer for them to grasp the principle that an 8c article along with 2c change together make up the same value as the 10c coin they had to begin with. So after you have given several students the opportunity to buy items and receive change, let the class tell you the various ways that ten can be partitioned into two sets.

Tell the students to look at the first example on Pupil Book page 80 and say what they see. (A 10c coin, a 5c price tag, a space to write the change and a number sentence to be completed.) Do the first example with the class and then allow them to complete the others on their own.

Units 77 and 78   Sorting shapes

Pupil Book pages 81 and 82

Materials
- a variety of cube, cuboid, spherical and cylindrical objects
- cardboard examples of solids

Objectives
Students should be able to:

- classify objects according to the three-dimensional shape they represent
- select and use their own criteria to classify three-dimensional shapes
- explain the criteria that they selected and used to classify a set of three-dimensional shapes.

Suggested approach

Display the cardboard solids that you have brought to class. Tell the class to imagine that they are in a giant supermarket, shopping for items of particular shapes. Show examples of solid shapes, and as you show each example, ask the class to try to think of as many items of that shape to add to the shopping trolley. Here are some possible suggestions:

- cube – boxes, playing blocks, cheese blocks, dice
- sphere – ball of cheese, tennis ball, melon, orange
- cuboid – tin of sardines, box of cereal, loaf of bread, cake tin
- cylinder – roll of wrapping paper, roll of gum, toilet paper, pipe

Read through page 81 of Pupil Book B with the students so they know what they have to do. Then ask them to complete the activity.

Show the students the cardboard solid shapes again. As a class describe the characteristics of each shape. For example the sphere and the cylinder have curved sides, the cube and the cuboid have straight sides.

Have a discussion about the difference between a cube and a cuboid. Accept answers such as: cuboids are longer than cubes, cuboids have some long sides, the sides of cubes are all squares, and so on.

Ask the students to complete page 82. Hopefully the students will group the shapes into cubes, cuboids and spheres. However, they should be able to explain to their partner why they grouped the shapes in the way that they did.

Unit 79 Looking back

Pupil Book page 83

> **Objectives**
> Students should be able to:
> - count in sets of 10
> - multiplying by 2, 3 and 4
> - represent one-quarter and one-half of a whole.

Suggested approach

This is a review lesson, which covers the skills and knowledge taught in the preceding units.

Read the instructions to the class. Let the students attempt the questions. Give guidance only as necessary. When the students have completed the Pupil Book page, discuss each of the questions and answers with them.

Note which students have difficulty and reinforce or reteach concepts as necessary.

Unit 80 How much have you learned?

Pupil Book page 84

> **Objectives**
> Students should be able to:
> - count in 10s
> - multiplying by 2, 3 and 4
> - represent one-quarter and one-half of a whole
> - read and write time on the hour and half hour
> - estimate lengths of objects using the metre as the unit of measure.

Suggested approach

This is an assessment lesson in which the students are tested on the concepts taught in the previous units.

Read the instructions to the class, so they all know what they have to do. When the students have completed the Pupil Book page, discuss each of the questions and answers with them.

Note which students have difficulty. You may want to give these students extra practice with these concepts.

Units 81 and 82   Test yourself

Pupil Book pages 85 and 86

> ### Objectives
> Students should be able to:
>
> deal with the key learning outcomes in this book.

Suggested approach

This is a review lesson, which covers all the key skills, knowledge and learning outcomes dealt with in this book.

Read the instructions to the class. Let the students attempt the questions. Give guidance only as necessary. When the students have completed the Pupil Book page, discuss each of the questions and answers with them.

Note which students have difficulty and reinforce or reteach concepts as necessary.

Unit 83   Assess yourself

Pupil Book page 87

Suggested approach

This page gives the students a chance to assess how well they think they did. What they enjoyed and what they found difficult. These pages will help you to assess which areas students need extra help with and in which areas you could extend the activities.

Glossary

acute angle	Any angle which measures between 0° and 90°.
acute triangle	Any triangle whose interior angles are all acute angles.
addition	The mathematical operation of finding the sum or total of two or more numbers. The sign for addition is +. For example, 17 + 3 = 20.
adjacent angles	Angles which have the same end point, and do not overlap.
angle	When two lines or line segments meet at a point, they form an angle. The amount of rotation from one line to another is called the angle.
arc	Part of a curve.
area	The size of a surface, measured in square units.
average	The sum of all the numbers divided by the number of elements in the set. For example, there is a group of six children. Their ages are 5, 8, 9, 10, 10, 12. The average age = $\frac{(5 + 8 + 9 + 10 + 10 + 12)}{6}$ = 9
axes	Lines which form the framework of a graph. Singular axis.
axis of symmetry	A line which divides a shape or image into symmetrical parts.
bar graph	A graph in which horizontal or vertical bars represent information.
billion	One thousand million or 10^9 (1 000 000 000).
BOMDAS	An acronym that helps students to remember the order of operations in a mixed sum. Operations within a sum or problem should be solved in this order: Brackets, Of, Multiplication, Division, Addition, Subtraction.
capacity	The interior volume of a container, or the volume it can hold.
chord	A line segment whose end points both touch points on a circle or curve.
circle	A plane shape formed by a curve on which all points are the same distance away from a centre point.
circumference	The curve that describes the boundary of a circle, or the length of this boundary.
composite number	A whole number which has more than two factors other than 1 and the number itself. For example, 2 × 3 = 6, so 6 is a composite number.
congruent	Having the same shape and size.
decimal	Relating to or using powers of ten or base ten. We can also refer to decimal fractions as decimals.
decimal fraction	A fraction written using place-value notation with base ten. The fraction is preceded by a dot, the decimal point. Each successive digit after the dot represents a multiple of the successive negative powers of ten. So 0.725 could be represented as $(7 \times 10^{-1})(2 \times 10^{-2})(5 \times 10^{-3})$, or in proper fractions as $^7/_{10}$ + $^{20}/_{100}$ + $^5/_{1000}$.

denominator	The number under the division line in a fraction. For example, 4 is the denominator in $3/4$.
diagonal	A line segment that joins two corners of a shape, but is not a side.
diameter of a circle	A chord that passes through the centre of the circle, or the length of a diameter.
element	One of the items in a set.
enlargement	An increase in the measure of a shape so that all sides and angles increase by the same proportion.
equivalent fractions	Two or more fractions which can be simplified to the same proper fraction. For example, $1/2$, $3/6$, $4/8$ and $6/12$ are all equivalent fractions.
exterior angle	An angle outside a plane shape, formed between a side of the shape and an extension of an adjacent side.
face	A plane surface of a three-dimensional shape.
factor	A number that divides exactly into another number. For example, 2 and 3 are factors of 6.
finite set	A set with a limited or defined number of members. For example, the set of even numbers between one and ten is a finite set.
highest common factor (HCF)	The highest number which divides into a given set of numbers exactly. For example, the HCF of 8 and 20 is 4.
improper fraction	A fraction which has a numerator which is a higher number than its denominator, for example, $11/2$ or $9/5$.
infinite set	A set with an unlimited or infinite number of members. For example, the set of even numbers is an infinite set.
intersecting sets	Two or more sets which have some members in common. The set of common members is also called the intersection of the sets.
interior angle	Angle inside a plane shape.
mean	Another word for average.
median	If we arrange a set of numbers in order, from smallest to largest, the median is the middle number, or numbers if there are an even amount in the set.
mixed number	A mixed number can be made of a combination of whole numbers and fractions. For example $51/2$ is a mixed number. If it is written as $11/2$, it is an improper fraction.
mode	The mode is the number that occurs most often in a set of numbers.
multiple	Any number that is the product of a given number and any another number. For example, 6, 9 and 12 are all multiples of 3.
numerator	The top line of a fraction, which is divided by the denominator. For example, 3 is the numerator of $3/4$.
obtuse angle	An angle which measures more than 90° and less than 180°.
parallel lines	Two (or more) lines on the same plane that never intersect.
perimeter	The boundary of a plane shape, or the length of this boundary.
prime factor	A factor which is a prime number. For example, 3 and 5 are the prime

factors of 15. A composite number can be expressed as the product of its prime factors.

radius	A line segment from the centre of a circle to its circumference. Plural radii.
prime number	A number which has only two factors – one and the number itself. For example, 13 only has two factors – 1 and 13.
probability	The likelihood that an event will happen.
proper fraction	A fraction which is less than one.
proportion	An equality between two ratios. The numbers 4 and 12 are in the same proportion as the numbers 1 and 3, because the fraction $^4/_{12}$ is equivalent to $^1/_3$.
ratio	A fraction used to compare two quantities of the same thing.
reflection	The movement of a shape when it is flipped over a line in its plane.
reflex angle	An angle which measures more than 180° and less than 360°.
right angle	An angle which measures 90°.
rotation	The movement of a shape about a point.
set	A well-defined collection of items or elements.
subset	A set within a set. For example, the set {vowels} is a subset of the set {letters of the alphabet}.
subtraction	The mathematical operation of finding the difference between two numbers. The sign for subtraction is –. For example 18 – 3 = 15.
symmetry	A shape has rotational symmetry if you can turn it about a point on to itself. A shape has line symmetry if you can fold or split the shape to create two mirror images.
translation	Movement of an object or shape so that all points move the same distance in the same direction.
Venn diagram	A diagram used to represent sets, using circles drawn around the elements of the set.
volume	The amount of space that an object takes up. We measure volume in cubic units.

Level 1 curriculum coverage grid

Pupil Book 1A

c = core   n = new objectives for this edition   e = extension

This grid will be updated in the event of future curriculum changes. For more information on the latest grid, please visit www.pearsoncaribbean.com.

Unit	Objectives	OECS*	Trinidad & Tobago	Bahamas	Barbados	Jamaica
Readiness activities	handle manipulatives in order to make patterns and sets	c	c	c	c	c
	manipulate sets of small objects to form patterns	c	c	c	c	c
	say the number words and count to three	c	c	c	c	c
	sort objects and put sorted objects into a specified place	c	c	c	c	c
	count to four	c	c	c	c	c
	put together sets of objects with and without instruction	c	c	c	c	c
	practise counting to five	c	c	c	c	c
	sort sets of objects	c	c	c	c	c
	work cooperatively	c	c	c	c	c
	count to six	c	c	c	c	c
	distinguish some simple shapes	c	c	c	c	c
	make sets containing many or few objects	c	c	c	c	c
	say which set contains more than or less than another	c	c	c	c	c
	count to eight	c	c	c	c	c
	match objects	c	c	c	c	c
	use the phrase 'as many as'	c	c	c	c	c
1	recognise the numerals from 1 to 5	c	c	c	c	c
	make sets representing the numerals 1 to 5	c	c	c	c	c
2	count in sequence up to six	c	c	c	c	c
3 and 4	use the numbers one to six confidently	c	c	c	c	c
	count to seven	c	c	c	c	c
5	use the numerals from 0 to 7 confidently	c	c	c	c	c
	count sets of objects up to seven	c	c	c	c	c
6	extend their knowledge of numerals and counting in sequence up to nine	c	c	c	c	c
7	extend their knowledge of numerals	c	c	c	c	c
	counting in sequence up to ten	c	c	c	c	c
	recognise the numeral for a given set	c	c	c	c	c
8 and 9	combine sets to make amounts to ten	c	c	c	c	c
	write number sentences to represent addition sums	c	c	c	c	c
10 and 11	apply their knowledge of combining sets to make ten or less	c	c	n	n	n
	review basic addition facts	c	c	c	c	c
	understand the commutative property of addition	c	c	c	c	c
12 and 13	identify the position of objects presented in concrete and pictorial form	c	e	n	c	n
	position objects according to descriptions of their relative positions	c	e	n	c	n
14	name the days of the week	c	e	n	c	n
	state the number of days in a week	c	e	e	c	c
15	name the months of the year	c	e	n	c	n
	state and write the current date of the current day	c	e	e	c	c
16	understand the concept of an empty set	c	c	c	c	c
	recognise and write 0	c	c	c	c	c
17 and 18	recognise the number sequence from zero to ten	c	c	c	c	c
	distinguish between odd and even numbers	c	c	c	c	c
	represent amounts on a number line	c	c	c	c	c
19	use the symbols > and = in number sentences	c	c	n	n	n
	add two one-digit numbers	c	c	n	c	n
	position objects according to descriptions of their relative positions	c	e	n	c	n
	name the days of the week	c	e	n	c	n
	name the months of the year	c	e	n	c	n
	state and write the date of the current day	c	e	e	c	c

*OECS includes Anguilla, Antigua & Barbuda, British Virgin Islands, Dominica, Grenada, Montserrat, St Kitts & Nevis, St Lucia, St Vincent & the Grenadines

Unit	Objectives	OECS*	Trinidad & Tobago	Bahamas	Barbados	Jamaica
20	identify the number of objects	c	c	n	c	n
	add two one-digit numbers	c	c	n	c	n
	identify the relative position of objects presented in pictorial form	c	e	n	c	n
	name the months of the year	c	e	n	c	n
21	make and match equal sets of objects	c	c	c	c	c
	use the word 'set' when referring to a group of objects	c	c	c	c	c
	use the = sign correctly and understand its meaning	c	c	c	c	c
22	begin to grasp the concept of 'one more than'	c	c	c	c	c
23	review 'one more than'	c	c	c	c	c
	begin to grasp the concept of 'one less than'	c	c	c	c	c
24	demonstrate their understanding of equal and unequal sets	c	c	c	c	c
	make sets according to given criteria	c	c	c	c	c
25 to 27	match objects in two sets to see which has more	c	c	c	c	c
	match objects in equal sets	c	c	c	c	c
	use the =, < and > signs correctly	c	c	c	c	c
28 and 29	develop further the concept of unequal sets	c	c	c	c	c
	practise making equal sets	c	c	c	c	c
	develop their concept of an empty set	c	c	c	c	c
30	recognise simple shapes	c	c	c	c	c
	use colours to classify objects	c	c	c	c	c
	recognise use of shapes in natural and human contexts	c	c	c	c	c
31	write the numerals from 1 to 5	c	c	c	c	c
	understand the meaning of each numeral	c	c	c	c	c
32	classify shapes	c	c	c	c	c
	present information on a bar graph	c	e	c	c	c
33	understand the concept of zero	c	c	c	c	c
	perform addition sums involving zero	c	c	c	c	c
34 and 35	recognise subtraction as a taking away process	c	c	c	c	c
	use the minus or subtraction sign (−)	c	c	c	c	c
	perform simple subtraction with numbers less than five	c	c	c	c	c
36	partition and combine sets of up to nine objects	c	c	c	c	c
37	recognise shapes	c	c	c	c	c
	write simple number sentences	c	c	c	c	c
38	recognise the number sequence from zero to ten	c	c	c	c	c
	represent amounts on a number line	c	c	c	c	c
	use a number line to add and subtract	c	c	c	c	c
39	demonstrate relationships among number facts for addition and subtraction	c	c	n	n	n
40	use the terms 'longer than', 'shorter than' and 'equal to'	c	c	c	c	c
	estimate and compare lengths sensibly	c	c	c	c	c
41	make and draw a set that is equal to, one more, or one less than a given set	c	c	n	n	n
	compare sets using the symbols, <, > and =	c	c	n	n	n
	add two one-digit numbers	c	c	n	c	n
42	select and use their own criteria to classify two-dimensional shapes	c	c	n	n	n
	add two one-digit numbers using objects and pictures/diagrams	c	c	n	c	n
	subtract a one-digit number using objects and pictures/diagrams	c	c	n	c	n
43	count from zero to ten	c	c	c	c	c
	write the numerals from 0 to 10	c	c	c	c	c
	complete and say the words for numbers from zero to ten	c	c	c	c	c
44 to 47	read and write numbers up to twenty in words and numerals	c	c	n	n	n
	count and identify the number of objects in a set of up to twenty objects	c	c	n	n	n
	make and draw sets of up to twenty objects	c	c	n	n	n
48	recognise the number sequence from zero to twenty	c	c	n	c	n
	represent amounts on a number line	c	c	c	c	c
49	identify number patterns	c	c	c	c	c
	sequence numbers to 20	c	c	c	c	c
50	use number names and write number sentences	c	c	c	c	c
51	make and draw a set that is equal to, one more than or one less than a given set	c	c	n	n	n

*OECS includes Anguilla, Antigua & Barbuda, British Virgin Islands, Dominica, Grenada, Montserrat, St Kitts & Nevis, St Lucia, St Vincent & the Grenadines

Level 1 curriculum coverage grid

Unit	Objectives	OECS*	Trinidad & Tobago	Bahamas	Barbados	Jamaica
52	present information on a bar graph	c	e	c	c	c
53	find numbers around them	c	c	c	c	c
	write the numerals 1 to 5	c	c	c	c	c
54 and 55	classify objects as heavy or light	c	c	c	c	c
	use a balance scale to measure and compare mass	c	c	c	c	c
56	apply the commutative law to simple addition sums	c	c	c	c	c
57	recognise the number sequence from zero to ten	c	c	c	c	c
	skip count on a number line to add one	c	c	c	c	c
58	perform simple addition sums	c	c	c	c	c
59 and 60	recognise the one-cent, five-cent, $1 and $5 coins	c	c	c	c	c
	add small coin amounts	c	c	c	c	c
	add money amounts up to five cents	c	c	c	c	c
61	name and recognise basic 2D shapes	c	c	c	c	c
	distinguish between squares and rectangles	c	c	c	c	c
62	identify and name rectangles and squares	c	c	n	c	n
	represent a coin value using several combinations of coins	c	c	n	c	n
	add 1	c	c	n	n	n
	read and write numbers up to twenty in numerals and words	c	c	n	n	n
	compare the mass of two objects	c	c	c	c	c
63	compare the mass of two objects	c	c	c	c	c
	make and draw a set that is equal to, one more or one less than a given set	c	c	n	c	c
	compare sets using the symbols <, > and =	c	c	n	n	c
	identify rectangles	c	c	n	c	c
	read and write numbers up to twenty in numerals and words	c	c	n	n	c
64	compare the size of sets using the number line	c	c	c	c	c
	use the symbols <, > and = ,	c	c	c	c	c
65 to 69	recognise and use numbers from 10 to 19	c	c	c	c	c
	break down numbers into tens and units	c	c	c	c	c
	combine sets of tens and units to make amounts to 19	c	c	c	c	c
70	name and recognise basic 2D shapes	c	c	c	c	c
71 to 73	use the concepts of longer than, shorter than, and equal lengths	c	c	c	c	c
	begin to estimate lengths	c	c	c	c	c
74	find the total value of a combination of coins	c	c	n	c	c
	combine smaller sets to make sets with up to nine objects	c	c	n	n	c
75	estimate the amount that a container can hold using informal units	c	c	c	c	c
	measure in informal units to check estimates	c	c	c	c	c
76	understand and use the terms 'full' and 'empty'	c	c	c	c	c
77	understand the concept of a fraction	c	n	n	c	c
78	cut and fold simple shapes to find a line of symmetry	c	e	c	e	c
	begin to explore simple halves	c	c	c	c	c
79 and 80	find half of a set of objects	c	c	c	c	c
81 and 82	recognise half of a single object	c	c	c	c	c
83	use the symbols <, > and = correctly	c	c	c	c	c
	identify one-half of a set	c	c	n	c	c
	determine the missing number in an addition number sentence	c	c	n	n	c
	add single digit numbers to 10	c	c	n	c	c
	compare the length of two objects using the words 'longer' and 'shorter'	c	c	c	c	c
84	compare the length of two objects using the words 'longer' and 'shorter'	c	c	c	c	c
	identify one-half of a set or an object	c	c	n	c	c
	determine the missing number in an addition number sentence	c	c	n	n	c
	subtract a one-digit number from numbers up to 20	c	c	n	c	c

*OECS includes Anguilla, Antigua & Barbuda, British Virgin Islands, Dominica, Grenada, Montserrat, St Kitts & Nevis, St Lucia, St Vincent & the Grenadines

Pupil Book 1B

c = core   n = new objectives for this edition   e = extension

This grid will be updated in the event of future curriculum changes. For more information on the latest grid, please visit www.pearsoncaribbean.com.

Unit	Objectives	OECS*	Trinidad & Tobago	Bahamas	Barbados	Jamaica
1 and 2	count in sequence to 50	c	e	n	c	n
3 to 6	extend partitioning to include sets of up to 20 objects	c	c	c	c	c
	draw missing sets and complete number sentences	c	c	c	c	c
7	subtract a one-digit number from numbers up to 20	c	c	n	c	n
8 and 9	name and recognise basic 2D shapes	c	c	c	c	c
	count items up to nine	c	c	c	c	c
	recognise shapes in the environment	c	c	c	c	c
	distinguish between squares and rectangles	c	c	c	c	c
10	use the terms 'lighter' and 'heavier' with confidence	c	c	c	c	c
	estimate which objects are 'lighter' or 'heavier' in a set	c	c	c	c	c
11 and 12	develop the skill of telling the time on the hour using both analogue and digital clocks	c	e	c	c	c
	relate time to their own activities	c	c	c	c	c
13	combine sets to make amounts to nine	c	c	c	c	c
14	name and combine coins up to ten cents	c	c	c	c	c
15 to 18	use ordinal numbers from first to tenth	c	c	c	c	c
	give the position of objects in an array	c	c	c	c	c
19	subtract a one-digit number from numbers up to 20	c	c	n	c	n
	use several devices and strategies to build up the basic number facts for addition and subtraction	c	c	n	c	n
	count in sequence to 50	c	e	n	c	n
	compare the mass of two objects using phrases such as 'heavier than', 'lighter than' etc	c	c	c	c	c
	tell the time on the hour	c	e	c	c	c
20	tell the time on the hour	c	e	c	c	c
	compare the mass of two objects using phrases such as 'heavier than', 'lighter than' etc	c	c	c	c	c
	use the symbols <, > and = correctly	c	c	c	c	c
	identify ordinal positions	c	c	n	n	n
	use several devices and strategies to build up the basic number facts for addition and subtraction	c	c	n	c	n
21	count in sequence to 50	c	e	n	c	n
22 to 25	count in 2s and 5s to 50	c	e	n	n	n
26 and 27	represent numbers and perform additions to 20	c	c	c	c	c
28	develop methods of adding three numbers	c	c	c	c	c
29	recognise odd and even numbers	c	c	c	c	c
	recognise and practise basic addition facts	c	c	c	c	c
30	subtract single-digit numbers from numbers between 11 and 20 using a number line	c	c	n	c	n
31	use a calculator to demonstrate relationships among number facts for addition and subtraction	c	e	n	c	n
32	use trial and error to investigate 2D shapes	c	c	c	c	c
33	explore patterns using regular shapes and environmental objects	c	c	c	c	c
	appreciate the idea of symmetry	c	e	c	e	e
34	read and interpret simple picture graphs	c	c	c	c	c
35	describe how data is presented in a bar graph	c	e	n	n	n
	read and interpret data represented in bar graphs	c	e	n	n	n
	describe similarities and differences between pictographs and bar graphs	c	e	n	n	n
36	measure length using body units	c	c	c	c	c
	understand why standard units are necessary	c	e		c	
37	estimate and measure the mass of objects using non-standard units	c	c	c	c	c
38	use combinations of coins to make totals up to 25c	c	c	c	c	c
39	interpret data represented in simple pictographs	c	c			
	compare the capacity of containers	c	c	c	c	c
	use objects to determine the missing number in an addition number sentence	c	c	n	n	n
	complete number patterns	c	c	c	c	c
40	interpret data represented in simple bar graphs	c	e	n	n	n
	compare the mass of objects using non-standard units	c	c	c	c	c
	count in twos	c	c	n	n	n
	use a number line to subtract two numbers	c	c	n	n	n
41	recognise and read number names to twenty	c	c	c	c	c
	match number names to given sets	c	c	c	c	c
42 and 43	count in sequence to 100	c	e	n	c	n

OECS includes Anguilla, Antigua & Barbuda, British Virgin Islands, Dominica, Grenada, Montserrat, St Kitts & Nevis, St Lucia, St Vincent & the Grenadines

Unit	Objectives	OECS*	Trinidad & Tobago	Bahamas	Barbados	Jamaica
44	use calculators to count in a variety of ways	c	e	n	c	n
45 to 48	use objects and pictures/diagrams to show repeated addition situations	c	c	n	n	n
	describe repeated addition situations using 'sets of'	c	c	n	n	n
	write number sentences to represent repeated addition situations	c	c	n	n	n
Unit 49	collect simple sets of data through simple interviews	c	c	n	n	n
	record collected data using simple number statements	c	c	n	n	n
50	describe the temperature of an object using phrases such as 'warm', 'hot', 'cold', etc.	c	e	n	n	n
51	understand and use the terms 'full' and 'empty'	c	c	c	c	c
	use standard units to measure capacity	c	c	c	c	c
	understand and use the term 'litres'	c	c	c	c	c
52	select the appropriate unit for measuring	c	c	c	c	c
53 and 54	use a balance scale to measure and compare mass	c	c			
	recognise and use the kilogram as a standard unit of mass	c	e	c	c	c
55 and 56	classify three-dimensional objects on the basis of their attributes, such as shape and/or size	c	c	n	c	n
	explain why a three-dimensional object can slide, roll or stack	c	e	n	n	n
57	represent a coin value (up to 20c) using several combinations of coins	c	c	n	c	n
58	combine and partition using coin amounts	c	c	c	c	c
	understand the concept of giving change	c	c	c	c	c
59	use number lines to count in 2s, 3s, 5s and 10s	c	n	n	n	n
60	identify which three-dimensional shapes can slide, roll or stack	c	e	n	n	n
	estimate the mass of objects using the kilogram as the unit of measure	c	e	n	n	n
	represent a coin value using several combinations of coins	c	c	n	c	n
61 and 62	count in 10s to 100	c	e	n	n	n
63 to 66	complete multiplication number statements, with products up to 16	c	c	n	n	n
	create and solve problems involving multiplication with products up to 16	c	c	n	n	n
67 and 68	recognise the metre (m) as a unit of measuring length	c	c	c	c	c
	estimate and measure lengths using standard units (m)	c	c	c	c	c
	record each of their estimates and measurements using the appropriate notation	c	c	n	n	n
69	understand the concept of half	c	c	c	c	c
	begin to explore the concept of symmetry	c	e	c	e	e
70 and 71	identify one half and one quarter of a whole	c	c	n	c	n
	represent one half and one quarter of a whole	c	c	n	c	n
	read and write the fractions $\frac{1}{2}$ and $\frac{1}{4}$	c	c	n	c	n
72 and 73	perform basic addition and subtraction	c	c	c	c	c
	recognise odd and even numbers	c	c	c	c	c
74 and 75	show how the hands of a clock move in relation to each other	c	c	c	c	c
	recognise and represent times on the hour and half-hour	c	e	c	c	c
76	combine and partition using coin amounts	c	c			
	understand the concept of giving change	c	c	c	c	c
77 and 78	classify objects according to the three-dimensional shape they represent	c	c	n	c	n
	select and use their own criteria to classify three-dimensional shapes	c	c	n	c	n
	explain the criteria that they selected and used to classify a set of three-dimensional shapes	c	c	n	n	n
79	count in sets of 10	c	e	n	n	n
	multiply by 2, 3 and 4	c	c	n	c	n
	represent one-quarter and one-half of a whole	c	c	n	c	n
80	count in 10s	c	e	n	n	n
	multiply by 2, 3 and 4	c	c	n	c	n
	represent one-quarter and one-half of a whole	c	c	n	c	n
	read and write time on the hour and half hour	c	e	c	c	c
	estimate lengths of objects using the metre as the unit of measure	c	c	c	c	c
81 and 82	deal with the key learning outcomes in this book	n	n	n	n	n

*OECS includes Anguilla, Antigua & Barbuda, British Virgin Islands, Dominica, Grenada, Montserrat, St Kitts & Nevis, St Lucia, St Vincent & the Grenadines